Other Brassey's titles

Godwin's Saga

A COMMANDO EPIC

by KENNETH MACKSEY

BRASSEY'S DEFENCE PUBLISHERS
(A member of the Pergamon Group)
LONDON · OXFORD · WASHINGTON · NEW YORK
BEIJING · FRANKFURT · SAO PAULO · SYDNEY · TOKYO · TORONTO

U.K. (Editorial)	Brassey's Defence Publishers, 24 Gray's Inn Road, London WC1X 8HR
(Orders)	Brassey's Defence Publishers, Headington Hill Hall, Oxford OX3 0BW, England
U.S.A. (Editorial)	Pergamon-Brassey's International Defense Publishers, 1340 Old Chain Bridge Road, McLean, Virginia 22101, U.S.A.
(Orders)	Pergamon Press, Maxwell House, Fairview Park, Elmsford, New York 10523, U.S.A.
PEOPLE'S REPUBLIC OF CHINA	Pergamon Press, Qianmen Hotel, Beijing, People's Republic of China
FEDERAL REPUBLIC OF GERMANY	Pergamon Press, Hammerweg 6, D-6242 Kronberg, Federal Republic of Germany
BRAZIL	Pergamon Editora, Rua Eça de Queiros, 346, CEP 04011, São Paulo, Brazil
AUSTRALIA	Pergamon-Brassey's Defence Publishers, P.O. Box 544, Potts Point, N.S.W. 2011, Australia
JAPAN	Pergamon Press, 8th Floor, Matsuoka Central Building, 1–7–1 Nishishinjuku, Shinjuku-ku, Tokyo 160, Japan
CANADA	Pergamon Press Canada, Suite 104, 150 Consumers Road, Willowdale, Ontario M2J 1P9, Canada

First edition 1987

Library of Congress Cataloging in Publication Data

Macksey, Kenneth.
Godwin's saga.
1. Godwin, John, d. 1945.   2. World War, 1939–1945 —
Commando operations.   3. Great Britain. Royal Navy —
Biography.   4. Seamen — Great Britain — Biography.
5. World War, 1939–1945 — Norway.   I. Title.
D794.5.G65M33   1987   940.54'5941   86-29893

British Library Cataloguing in Publication Data

Macksey, Kenneth
Godwin's saga: a commando epic.
1. World War, 1939–1945 — Commando
operations   2. Great Britain — Armed
Forces — Commando troops
I. Title
940.54'12'41   D794.5

ISBN 0-08-034742-8

Printed in Great Britain by A. Wheaton & Co. Ltd., Exeter

Contents

List of Illustrations

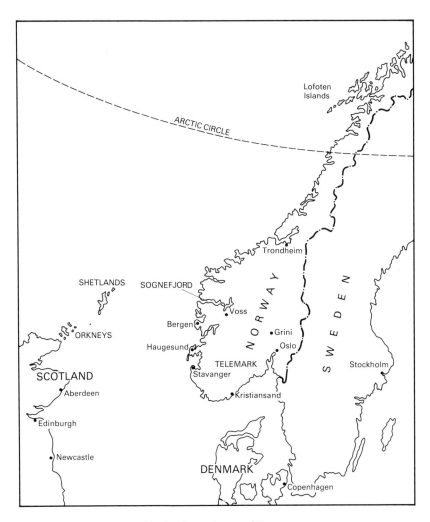

FIG 1.   Strategic map of Norway

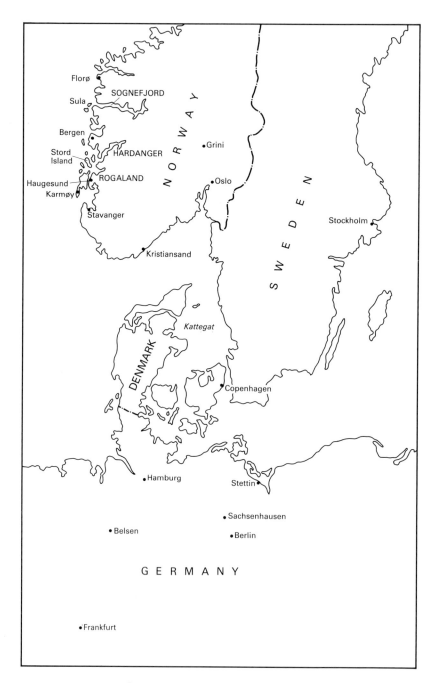

FIG 2. Area covered in Godwin's travels

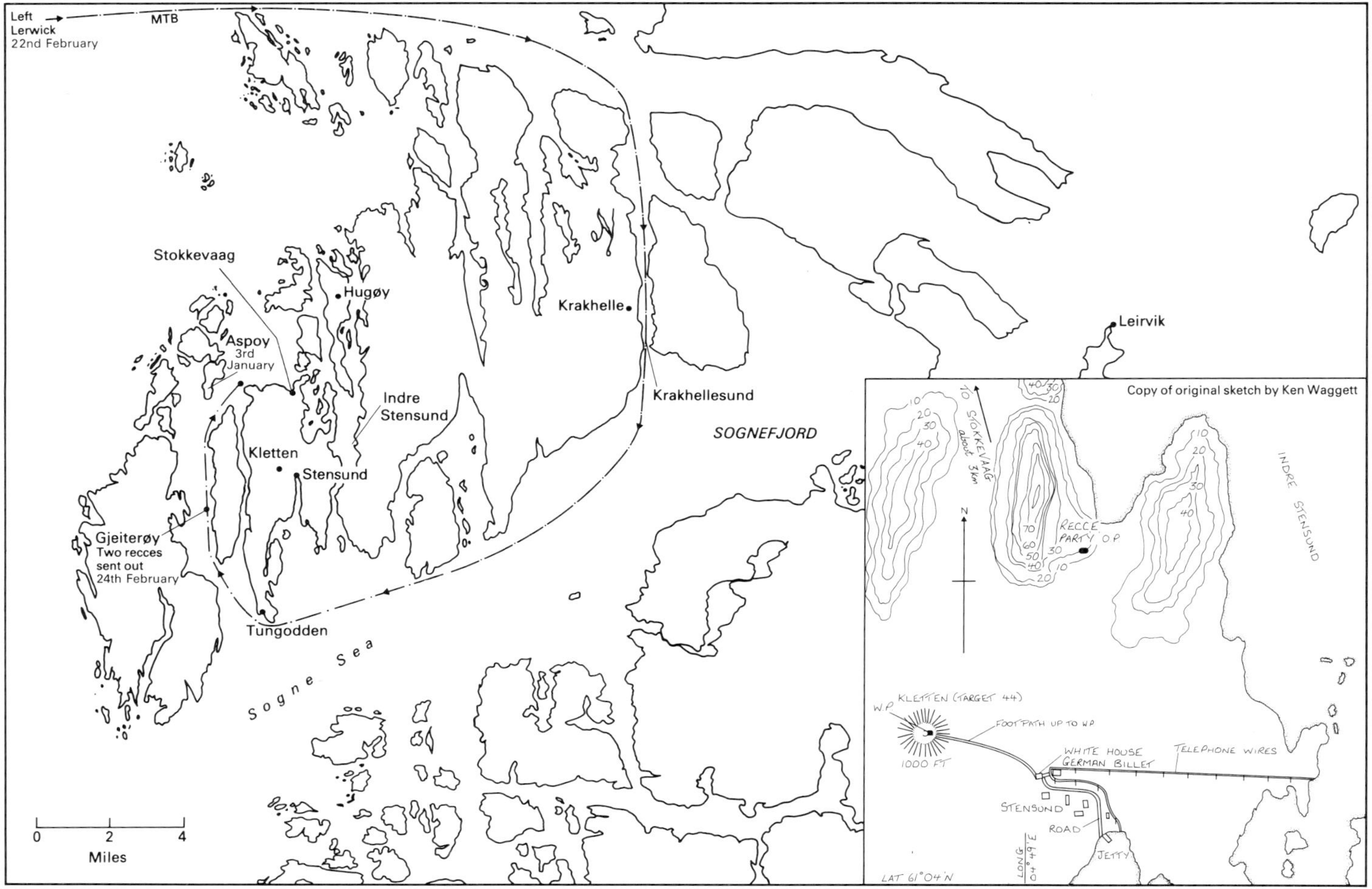

Fig 3. Operation CRACKERS

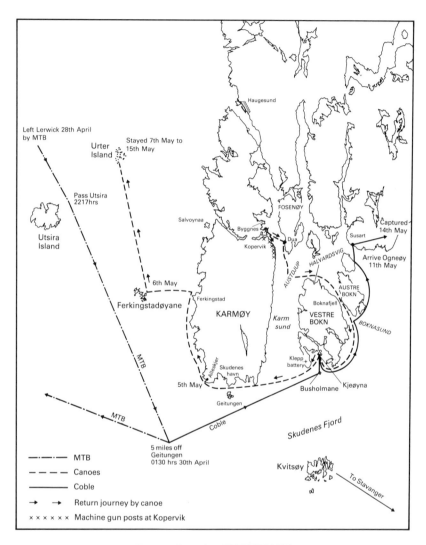

Fig 4. Operation CHECKMATE

Prologue

In the winter of 1942/43, at the turning point of the Second World War, Norway lay at the mercy of the occupying German forces, the depredations of an illegal government in Oslo under Vidkun Quisling, and harrying by forces sent from Britain to raid the coastline. The first consideration of a population, whose predominant loyalties were given to the king and government in exile in Britain, was usually focused upon survival in the face of terror from the German Gestapo, SS and Wehrmacht. But they also lived in some dread of what horrors their own hotheaded Resistance saboteurs might unleash or what blows the British might strike at the enemy in their midst. Keen as the mass of the people were to see the back of the Germans, they had, in the aftermath of invasion in April 1940, taught themselves to live, let live and even, among a shrewd entrepreneural few, to prosper with a foot in both camps. In learning how to live with oppression, many Norwegians had come to dread raiding forces which had a nasty habit of bringing in their train dire retribution from the Germans. In the minds of average citizens lurked a desire to withhold outright resistance until the time was ripe—meaning the day when the enemy would be overcome easily at minimal cost in lives and property. That was not an exclusive Norwegian attitude—the trait was common to nearly all occupied countries.

Yet in that grim winter, as the Germans, ever fearful of an invasion, tightened their grip on Norway and feverishly constructed fortifications the length of the heavily indented coastline, the people began to stir in the realisation Germany was losing the war. As Quisling's acolytes began to fear the future and waverers changed direction towards positive positions of resistance for the future on the king's side—'rowing' as it came to be known—the coastline, and several isolated spots in the interior, began to seethe with hostilities. Where in the first two years of war, landings by British naval and air forces, commando troops and agents had been few and far between, hardly a night now passed but the throb of muffled engines, the thud of torpedoes, the thump of bombs or the bark of guns disturbed the composure of the irresolute and stimulated the belligerence of the undaunted. By submarine, motor-torpedo boat (MTB), and fishing boat they came and went by sea, with the occasional party slipping in by parachute or glider and out via Sweden. In fjord and dale the saboteurs lurked while agents infiltrated the populace, delving for information, organising resistance, distributing arms and explosives and blowing up vital installations.

Brave men from many nationalities risked their lives in this clandestine, hit-and-run ferment. The fishing boats of the so-called Shetland Bus (which trafficked in agents, escaping patriots, arms and explosives), along with the majority of MTBs stalking shipping in the Inner Leads and fjords, were manned by Norwegians, who had escaped to fight on. Norwegians also were to be found among air crew, commando parties and as agents returned to live subversively among their own people. Rubbing shoulders with this nucleus of Norwegians was also to be found, in addition to a majority of British, the Alliance in microcosm—Canadians, Eskimos, Red Indians and Americans, to name but the most prominent. They assembled, for the most part, in north Scotland and the Orkneys and Shetland Islands where the mingling of dedicated fighting men with the hardy local populace compounded an explosive force of almost unique composition. Here several navies' blue uniforms (embellished by the red pompoms atop Norwegian sailors' hats), the multitude of distinguishing shoulder flashes on khaki battle dress or light blue air force jackets, and a mélange of accents, dialects and languages, coalesced into a community whose sole purpose was to inflict harm on the Germans in Norway. It was a strange amalgam of quite small, specialist groups, set apart from the masses who comprised the fleets and armies which would eventually bring Germany to her knees. These were the trail blazers of major invasions, individualists and mavericks to the fore. Among whom was to be found John Godwin, a determined, yet at times diffident, young officer of the Royal Naval Volunteer Reserve who had left Argentina to take part in the war and whose chosen method of entering Norway, land of the sagas, was by MTB, coble and canoe.

1

The Saboteur from
Buenos Aires

There is nothing among the rolls of ancestry to indicate direct lineage connecting John Godwin of Buenos Aires with the mighty Earl Godwin of Wessex and Kent who held sway over England during the reign of Edward the Confessor. Nor would it be right to equate the story of the twentieth-century bearer of the appellation with an illustrious namesake about whom sagas were told. Yet both in their ways generated a folklore of heroism which transcends history by entering the annals of legend. And while the mighty Earl spent most of his life in the eleventh century steeped in war, the much lowlier John had to wait until his twentieth year before witnessing the flash of battle.

As one of twins born on 13 December 1919, John Godwin belonged to a family which had been engaged in management of a ranch in Argentina since the first decade of the century. He grew up in touch with two of the main forces which inexorably shaped his saga—the sea and the indigenous Germans of Buenos Aires. The sea bore upon it the ships and small craft which stirred his spirit of adventure. The German community and, more than ever, Germans who were contaminated in the 1930s by Nazism, figured within the all-pervasive environment of commercial and political rivalry. Neither influence could he have avoided had he wished. Like the youths of the Houses of Montague and Capulet, the sons of the British and German merchants, who vied for trade and influence in cosmopolitan Buenos Aires, carried their families' rivalries and their nation's quarrels into school and onto the streets. To Godwin's generation, the unforgotten, though unexperienced, enmities of a previous war loomed large. At home they sensed the jealousies inherent in Argentinian trade preference granted to Britain in return for a guaranteed export market for beef, and they resented the provocative sight of an Argentinian Army equipped and trained to look like its German model.

John Godwin and his twin brother Peter were brought up in the 100 per cent British tradition and were educated in England, between 1928 and 1938, latterly at Malvern College. He enjoyed games, was average at soccer and

1

tennis and a good batsman at cricket. But one phrase predominated and recurred in his housemaster's reports—he was a born leader of men. Their last years at school coincided, of course, with the intensifying European crisis with its background of broken treaties, invasions, racial oppression and reports about concentration camps and the conditions in camps which to those who had not seen them were unimaginable. It cannot be said that, as a result of this, Godwin came, at this stage, to hate Germans in the true sense of that word. For one thing, he was not the sort who would willingly contemplate killing. Simply, he became aware of a situation which made war against Germany more than likely, one in which his education and natural conscience would forbid him to stand aside from.

When war did break out on 1 September 1939, repercussions were bound to be felt in Argentina. No doubt the Montagues and Capulets possessed similar feelings to Nazi Party-orientated German youth groups and the British Fellowship of the Bellows. They wore distinguishing badges and brawled in public; and the twentieth-century versions went just a little further by collecting funds for their own nation's war effort and yearning for the day when they could take ship for Europe to join the main fight. It was all fairly harmless until the day of Godwin's twentieth birthday when reports, astutely circulated by the Germans to the newspapers, ahead of all others, and tilted regardless of the truth, proclaimed a notable German naval victory in nearby waters. The pocket battleship *Admiral Graf Spee*, it was said, had sunk three British cruisers and triumphantly was entering Montevideo harbour on the Uruguayan side of the River Plate. Shock, mitigated only by instinctive disbelief, gave the British community several bad hours while the Germans celebrated ecstatically. But as John Godwin would later learn for himself, rumours and, in particular, German manufactured rumours of outright victory or defeat, were frequently subject to amendment—in this case quite substantial amendment once it became clear that the British squadron was intact, if damaged, and that it had been substantially reinforced. Or so British manufactured rumours stated, as the moment for the *Graf Spee*'s departure from her neutral haven approached and the prospect loomed of a naval battle just outside the three-mile limit.

Like spectators of ancient Rome swarming to the Colosseum, the crowds packed the ferries from Buenos Aires to Montevideo, shoulder to shoulder in rival anticipation of *Graf Spee*'s destiny. Puzzled, they saw through binoculars, or heard as the Godwins did from the excited radio commentators, of inexplicable goings on. About sailors disembarking shortly before the ship was due to sail, and a general air of mystery. Intrigued, the crowds watched her move slowly down stream, battle ensign flying but guns trained fore and aft in a most unbattleworthy alignment. Amazed, they noticed that she had veered from the main channel and had come to anchor in shallow waters. By the light of the setting sun, craft came and went alongside until a stillness settled upon her which disclaimed expectancy. Dramatically came the answer to their questions, even as the keener eyed began to imagine she was sitting lower in the water. Instead of the flash of guns there came an eruption of flame from below decks, engulfing her in smoke, before the funereal thunder of her magazines's exploding rolled across the water. They had witnessed a symbolic event, the ritual scuttling of a German ship to prevent its loss to the enemy, a humiliation soon linked to the suicide by shooting of its much respected Captain Langsdorf. Events such as these made an impression on men such as John Godwin to whom ships were beautiful, demanding of respect. He could no more approve the immolation of the *Graf Spee* and her captain than abide the violence and excesses of the Nazi regime — or recognise the slightest possibility of the Royal Navy losing the battle at Montevideo. The war and the Navy beckoned.

Like most young people of British descent, the Godwin twins were anxious to join the Allied armed forces as soon as possible. But as apprentices in commerce and, more to the point, of an age group liable for military service in the Argentine forces, even after the twins had negotiated a special exemption, they could not, as reservists, leave the country while their age group was serving without laying themselves open to charges of desertion, and hazarding their postwar careers in Argentina. Moreover, there was no immediate need for them in Britain where the armed forces were ill-prepared to receive their own nationals, let alone volunteers from overseas. So it was not until early in 1941 that, at last, the twins were free to take passage in a fast ship of the Houlder line, having recently celebrated their twenty-first birthdays, and knowing that by this time their services would be welcome in Britain. But with their parents' feelings in mind, they deliberately joined separate Services to obviate any possibility of becoming casualties among the company of the same ship, regiment or squadron. Peter joined the Army because John was determined to join 'his beloved Royal Navy'.

The voyage to Britain, out of convoy, was in itself an education and a preparation for John in the task ahead. He was able to come to understand, first hand, how a large, fast vessel could (they all hoped) avoid U-boats and enemy aircraft by losing itself in the boundless ocean's spaces, making full use of the long winter's Arctic nights off Iceland. Yet queasily aware that if sunk and cast adrift in those frigid waters the chances of death from hypothermia were as sure as could be. Learning, too, from hours spent on the bridge and the poop with the Royal Marines gunner, how to strip, assemble, lay and fire the anti-aircraft machine-guns, the 40-mm Bofors and the 6-in gun — sometimes with the sneaking wish that a hostile target would present itself for target practice of a deadly kind. As a result, the young man who presented himself for drill, physical training and basic instruction at the shore station called HMS *Collingwood* was almost a ready-made ordinary seaman fit to join a fighting ship as an anti-aircraft gunner.

Godwin was in a hurry to go to war, his anxiety on this score hastened by the

Royal Navy which usually made Latin American volunteers serve a spell on the lower deck before putting forward men of obvious officer qualities, such as Godwin, for a commission.

It may have been too, at this stage, that this slim, bespectacled, grey-eyed young man would have elected to acquire more knowledge of the ordinary sailor. For one thing, it was not in his character to impose himself. He tended sometimes to withdraw unpretentiously into his shell when face to face with dominant people—only to erupt somewhat unpredictably when prevented from having his way. Whatever the reason for his remaining an ordinary seaman, soon upgraded to able seaman, it was to take him into action with the least delay on board one of the most celebrated warships afloat, the aircraft carrier HMS *Ark Royal* whose fame in action was almost equalled by her notoriety in frequent German claims to have sent her to the bottom.

Manning one of *Ark Royal*'s multi-0.5-in anti-aircraft machine-gun batteries gave him a thrill in action, even though the chances of doing much harm to the enemy were low. The true joy of being in the carrier was living among the sailors and coming to love their camaraderie, a moving experience he never forgot and which was to prove of immense value in the hard times to come. But this was a transitory phase in his life, insufficient to a person whose urge was to hurt the enemy in person—a function which, so far as he could see, was mainly the prerogative of a few privileged aircrew manning the 72 flying machines carried by the 22,000-ton ship. In her sorties from Gibraltar, into the Mediterranean and the Atlantic, it had been the airmen who had won true fame for *Ark Royal*, above all from one lucky torpedo hit which had made all the difference between the escape or destruction of the mighty German battleship *Bismarck*.

Being an insignificant part of an enormous complex with little chance of making a really personal contribution to the war made him dissatisfied. It was the air crew he envied, they who struck the vital blows and made a personal contribution with a single weapon, deliberately aimed. That was a lot different to spraying bullets aloft, in company with scores of other gunners, hoping, by a chance in a thousand, to inflict minor damage which might, just might, lead to fatal consequences for the enemy. It was the sensation of impotence which, in the autumn of 1941, made him seek a change—that and the sheer grinding monotony of existence in a big ship among 1600 other men.

Godwin learned about monotony on the mess decks, how ship's jargon, like mess-deck conversation, was repetitive, along with the food, which was also repetitive and none too appetising at times. The same old catch-phrases, jests, vulgarities at which he had laughed at first and come to repeat as a member of the crowd, eventually sounded stale and became just another facet of the over-bearing monotony. Action's brief excitements could and did alleviate boredom in the instant, but was invariably interwoven with fear which, unlike most other impulses, was extremely difficult to share with shipmates, most of whom erected a barrier of small talk and banter to hide their inner feelings. *Ark*

Royal was his university where he studied shipmates with care and with profit. Gradually he understood their simplicity in insistence upon food, sleep and women, in no particular order but in regular quantities, and thus discovered what uplifted or cast them down; how to appeal to their senses of duty, patriotism and comradeship without seeming to be patronising. To his surprise he found that pride in ship was qualified, and frequently took second place in loyalty to much smaller groups such as mess deck or gun crew. There were even quite a number who cursed the famous ship as a steel tyrant driven remorselessly by either an ambitious Captain or an insensitive Admiralty. Beneath the ratings' willingness to serve, he detected a ground swell of anxiety; a yearning for a change from Gibraltar, with its social limitations; and to be back home with their women, their families and in the public houses where they might, within the restrictions of security, boast just a little about their adventures, and let off more steam than they could on board.

So when the U-81's torpedo struck *Ark Royal* amidships at tea time on 13 November 1941 and she began rapidly to list, there were among the crew those who took heart in the hope of a spell in dockyard, a break in the old routine. And others, like John Godwin, for whom the explosion was a career's turning point. For when at last the initial shouting had died down, and the ship's engines had been stopped to prevent her driving to destruction as water poured in, it became fairly obvious that *Ark Royal* was in dire straits. It was a relief when action stations were ordered by word of mouth and bugle and he could run to his post above the flight deck through semi-darkness and flickering lights. Top sides he saw smoke pouring from the vents and judged that, unless immediate counter-flooding took place, she might soon roll over as another carrier had done in similar circumstances. Watching a destroyer coming alongside was a relief, as word was passed for all but 250 or so essential crew members to be taken off.

In darker days to come, Godwin's story of the last hours of *Ark Royal* would entertain his comrades vastly. He told a tale well, although not the detailed saga of how, for over 12 hours, the party left aboard fought might and main to save the ship and bring her safely to Gibraltar a mere 30 miles distant. He was among those chosen to depart at once and thus able to observe and catch the mood of those waiting to jump perilously onto a bed of hammocks laid thick upon the destroyer's foredeck. Afterwards he relished the absurdities of the situation as more than one thousand people emerged from below, each clutching cherished possessions, moving in an orderly way to the ship's side and praying she would stay upright just long enough to let them get off. He recalled the Paymaster being cheered as he carried a suitcase stuffed with money; and sailors, their pockets bulging with worthless trinkets which, on the spur of the moment, had assumed a compelling sentimental value; and he noticed a general tendency to save presents for those at home, such rarities in the shops as clothing and, above all, silk stockings. Some might laugh when he mentioned that wild leap from flight deck to destroyer with its fear of injury from falling upon the next man ahead or being struck by the ones behind. But in a later setting, the mirth would change to reflection when he spoke of the squalor and apprehension on board that destroyer packed with ten times her normal complement as she returned to her duties in the escort. Listeners who were enslaved to conditions of squalor and apprehension which were inconceivable, recognised then what he was saying; in grim circumstances, hope must never be lost. How *Ark Royal*'s crew fought to keep her afloat, great survivor as she was, until finally she had to be abandoned. Only then would he relax and, with a wry chuckle, mention some among those watching *Ark Royal* cling to life, line the rail and shout 'Sink you bastard! Sink.'

Shortly after returning to Gibraltar, his application for a commission was approved. He came to England for a course at HMS *King Alfred* and, on 26 March 1942, emerged, resplendent in a smart new uniform with the single, thin wavy gold stripes on its sleeves—Sub-Lieutenant John Godwin, RNVR, tempered and ready to rejoin the war. A different war, nevertheless, from the one he may have envisaged when first he took ship from Buenos Aires; one involving small boats, and explosives in knowledge of which he was a novice. For at *King Alfred*, Godwin had taken a very deliberate step by volunteering for Combined Operations, complying with the blandishments of Vice-Admiral Lord Louis Mountbatten who, as Chief of Combined Operations, had dangled before the cadets the attractions of immediate command of a small craft as opposed to subservience in a larger ship. Bowing also to the strictures of his instructor in navigation who, after blanching at his student's appalling results in learning the rudiments of that subject, cried, 'Godwin, you must never sail out of sight of land, because if you do, you and your crew will become lost and that's a certainty.'

With that in mind, John Godwin arrived at Hayling Island and accidentally became a saboteur.

2

The Buccaneer from Norway

As a trainee sub-lieutenant of the Royal Norwegian Navy, Charles Herlofson was thrust onto a converging course with John Godwin by the bark of guns at 4 a.m. on 9 April 1940. Through thick fog from his bedroom window overlooking Horten Harbour, near the mouth of the Oslo Fjord, he saw but little of the fight as a Norwegian minelayer and a midshipman's training vessel opened fire upon several fast craft attempting to land. But although astonished, surprised he was not. The flash and racket of battle was logically consistent with a half-hearted state of alert which had been called the day before. This violence simply meant that persistent rumours of impending invasion had come true—and in Herlofson's mind there resided little doubt as to who the invaders were. Certainly not the British, whom he trusted, despite their incursions into Norwegian waters and announcement of intention to lay mines in Norway's Inner Leads to hamper the movement of iron ore ships from Narvik to Germany. Like everybody else, he had read the newspaper reports about the sinking off Pillesand, by a submarine, of the large German ship *Rio de Janeiro*: how terrified horses had been spotted in the chill sea; and how the rescued German soldiers had admitted they had been on their way to protect Norway from English invaders.

History also guided Herlofson to his conclusions and had been the subject he was studying past midnight for an exam, that day, he would never sit. It told him that the British were not in the least likely, unprovoked or uninvited, to land upon Norwegian soil. On the other hand, history did not rule out invasion by Germany, bearing in mind her recent past record and the instincts of most Norwegian sailors who recalled with bitterness the arrogant destruction of their shipping by German U-boats in the last war, when Norway had succeeded, with monetary profits and high cost, in staying neutral.

Young men of action like Herlofson are not renowned for taking full account of all the factors of a problem. They reject caution and in Norway would be among those who, in the future, lamented their country's weakness. The angry young men, and some who were not so young, could not excuse the timidity of their government in taking only half-hearted measures against clear evidence of an imminent threat from Germany; or leaders who pointed out that Norway had benefitted from keeping clear of wars since 1814. They despised the habits of a long peace which seemed immutably cloying of the combative spirit.

Fiercely, in after years, the critics could cite the 65-year-old Colonel Erikson who, as commander of the Oscarborg fortress guarding the Drøbak Narrows in the Oslo Fjord, had implacably rejected the vacillation of his superior officer at a moment of supreme crisis. What might have been the outcome, they asked, if he had obeyed the order to leave unmolested the big German cruiser *Blücher* as she steamed unannounced and unwanted towards a capital city where the majority of whose defending officers slept after being sent home the previous evening? Supposing he had held his hand instead of slapping two torpedoes along with a salvo of shells into the interloper? Would the legend of Norwegian resistance in the years to come, and based upon the stubborn independence of tough individuals, have looked the same—or even been written? Certainly not, said the patriots, and not simply because the spectacle of the great ship rolling over in flame and smoke to decant more than a thousand soldiers and sailors into the icy waters acted as an inspiration to those of aggressive intent. The interception, along with the fog which delayed the arrival of additional German troops, had saved Oslo from early capitulation and given the Storting sufficient time in which to grant King Haakon and the government plenary powers before they escaped inland. That was why Norway, it was claimed with pride, did not emulate her sister nation Denmark in bending at once and at the same time to German will, and why Herlofson and all those of his persuasion legally carried on the fight in the years ahead. And that, also, was why Vidkun Quisling, a failed Storting candidate and leader of the minority Nasjonal Samling Party, won only scanty support when the Germans set him up as head of a puppet regime.

Independent of mind as many people were, they also had a preference for properly vested authority. Truth, however, would emerge only gradually to Herlofson and fellow officers to whom all was chaos amid reports that Kristiansand, Stavanger, Bergen, Trondheim and Narvik—the country's main ports—were in German hands. Meanwhile, they and their superiors suffered from the ennui which took its toll at the higher levels plus the absence of a plan to meet a totally unexpected situation. When attempts to move the sixty sub-lieutenants up country fell apart in an atmosphere of doubt, hopelessness overcame anger, pride and duty. The order instructing the officers to disperse to their homes or do whatever they liked to serve their country as best they could, was merely one aspect of that initial defeatism in adversity.

Most young Norwegians then, as now, were fit and bold, as befitted a nation of seamen who, in the depths of winter, lived for skiing. Given that they reached peaks of physical fitness, and all the more so if they were, like

Herlofson, one of the élite band of high ski-jumpers, they tended to look for a fight. Disarmed, without a ship in which to serve, Herlofson and three like-minded sub-lieutenants boarded a train for Bergen 'in the hope and belief that we might be able to offer our knowledge of Norwegian coastal waters to British naval ships—which *we* believed *must* be hunting the German ships'—as indeed they were with mixed success and failure. Unerringly they headed in the direction of the fighting, until they reached the up-land town of Voss where despondency again prevailed. Bergen was firmly in German hands, they were told. An assembly of generals and naval officers were debating what to do with a motley collection of blue jackets and soldiers, 'plus the four of us sub-lieutenants'.

A week later Herlofson received his first command after helping set up an organisation to secure the mighty Sognefjord, Norway's longest fjord with its high rocky walls rearing stark from the deep black waters, and its minute communities farming the sparse fields and seeking the superabundance of fish upon which survival traditionally most depend. Here, where the loudest sound was the tonk tonk of the fishing boats' heavy diesel engines, Herlofson put to sea in a small fishing boat with one civilian to tend the engine and a single blue jacket to man 0.5-in Colt machine-gun. In retrospect, it emerges as a strange coincidence that his introduction to war was in surroundings which in due course he would visit with Godwin, but in a considerably more powerful craft than the one in which he was now embarked. It was also educational. A master's exam behind one and a Merchant Marine mate's certificate in your pocket are not the best qualifications for indulgence in combat against a wily and overwhelming foe among narrow inlets, rocky outcrops and steep fell sides. A soldier's or hunter's training is better suited to that, and a strategy of hide and seek, not fiery confrontation, the only practical manner of making even a faint impression without committing suicide. Gradually these facts were drawn to Herlofson's attention after beginning his optimistic mission, but brought home with a rush when he took station at the mouth of the fjord while visiting Sula, Leirvik and the several other places which would become so familiar and important later on unforgettable occasions. For here he met the local shooting club, armed to the teeth, anxious to fight but unversed in tactics, who expected this young naval officer to take command and provide the wisdom they lacked.

A rapidly deteriorating military situation and, it has to be added, a measure of good fortune, ordained that Herlofson and his amateur soldiers were denied the opportunity to test their rudimentary skills. Against professionals their moment of glory would have been short indeed, as was so much Norwegian resistance against the powerful German thrust which quickly overran the southern provinces. The thin defences of the Sognefjord had to lapse into irrelevance as the fighting moved north to centre upon the Anglo-French bridgeheads at Trondheim, Namsos and Narvik, just as the whole defence of

Norway became hopeless once those bridgeheads were penned in and compelled to withdraw. With thousands of compatriots, Herlofson again found himself redundant in defence of his country, compelled to choose between surrender to the enemy or hiding his uniform to merge with the population and await the next call to make fuller use of his skills. In the meantime the picture of the Sognefjord was locked away in his memory, a clear record of suitable hiding places, commanding topographical features, unique tidal conditions and strong currents in this important waterway's mouth.

From hiding he witnessed and experienced his country's pangs of creeping oppression after the Allies and his own government had withdrawn to Britain in June. He learnt about the overrunning of Holland, Belgium and France and shared the gloom of Norwegians who, momentarily, began to lose faith in their future as the German Army Command put its weight behind Vidkun Quisling and as the apparatus of the SS *Sicherheitsdienst* (SD) security organisation and the *Geheime Staatspolizei* (Gestapo) infiltrated the state system. All round lay the corrosion of doubt, stimulated by Quisling's wheedling and the seductively soft touch of the occupation authorities insidiously rotting the fabric of old. A corrupt fragmentation drove the bureaucracy and the police to behave unnaturally to simulate impartiality in an environment of partiality, as it encouraged industrialists and merchants to profiteer from lucrative opportunities and undermined the judgement of citizens suffering from shock, dismay and apathy. Among them were more than a few unbiased Norwegians who conceded that some Germans were quite decent people, particularly when they tried so hard to be liked. After all, the Germans suggested, you Norwegians and we Germans are of the Nordic race and of the same—well almost the same—purity. Why should we not be friends and comrades in arms? Repudiate a king and government who have left you in the lurch. Take to your hearts the compatriots who have stayed to help you. Reject the foolish handful among you who fatuously refuse to speak German which we know is the first language in your schools, or pretend they cannot understand us when we speak Norwegian.

Some conclusive historic events passed unnoticed at the time, but not the Storting's resolve to reject the recommendation of its presidential board, to repudiate the king and government in exile in favour of the despised pretender Quisling. It was said next day that people held their heads high again and that their linguistic intransigence took a turn for the extreme. It was also observed that the Germans were astonished as well as disappointed in their under-estimation of Norwegian spirit; but their appointment of Reichscommissioner Joseph Terboven and the issue of a stream of edicts and manifestations of SS-backed security measures marked an end to the honeyed words. Even decent Germans became harsh and noisy as the minions of enforcement carried out sudden arrests, brusque interrogations and the rounding up of dissident people. As prisons, such as Grini, began to fill up, the tension heightened and resistance became more popular if inept. It takes more than a month to learn

PLATE 1. John Godwin

PLATE 2.   Sergeant Jack Cox of 12 Commando

PLATE 3.   Neville Burgess

PLATE 4.   Keith Mayor

PLATE 5. Ken Waggett (*pointing*) with Lord Mountbatten after the war

about clandestine warfare after more than a century's peace. But the Norwegians were willing to learn—and helped to do so, gradually, by a network of internal communication with tentacles reaching out from their government in Britain.

After five months, one of those tentacles touched Charles Herlofson whose willingness to resist was stronger than ever, but whose talents were deemed better employed professionally at sea rather than on land tormenting the Germans until the inevitable happened and he was caught and thrown into gaol. Towards the end of November, with three older naval officers (one of whom later would become Chief of Norwegian Defence Forces), the future Rear Admiral Herlofson made his way to Aalesund and, dressed as a fisherman, headed for the Shetland Isles (Norwegian territory until 1469) in a small fishing boat powered by a defective engine. The four-day voyage was to be a minor epic in itself, the meticulously kept log telling of freezing cold winds and mountainous seas which repeatedly threatened to overwhelm the little boat—as it quite frequently did to some other patriots on the run as they made for a new life. But like true Norsemen this determined party, overcoming all hazards, including a complete engine failure, entered harbour at 1340 hours, 8 December ready to rejoin their navy where it sailed under command of their king and government in the continued fight against Germany.

At this consummation some ambitious officers might have rested content. At 597 tons, with three 4-in and one 40-mm AA gun and two 21-in torpedo tubes and a crew of 72, *Sleipner* was a compact fighting vessel with nothing like the impersonality found in an aircraft carrier. She would spend most of her time at sea, escorting convoys, seeking U-boats and, in due course, playing her part in raids by daring bands of commandos who began to make life unpleasant for the Germans defending the coastline of Europe. But not for Herlofson such prolonged monotony of endless hours watch-keeping with hardly a sight of the enemy and without the ultimate responsibility of command. Boredom, which could stifle the uninspired and indolent or inspire extrovert characters to deeds of valour, sharpened his thirst for action just when it became known that the Royal Norwegian Navy was forming a flotilla of the latest MTBs for the purpose of carrying the war to the enemy in the most delectable manner imaginable—right among the coastal waters of the homeland itself. It was a measure of his reputation, as one of the buccaneering kind, that from among a shoal of applications, his name came out in August 1942 along with promotion to Lieutenant and eventually, ecstasy of ecstasies, command of MTB 619. Nameless she might be, and a mere 95 tons, but when he looked from her bridge upon the two torpedo tubes, with their 21-in missiles, and the sinister black muzzles of 57-mm cannon and machine-guns, pointing fore and aft, he ruminated that her striking power was almost as much as *Sleipner*'s. It was almost too good to be true.

3

The Chief from 1A Richmond Terrace

As a consequence of having influenced John Godwin to volunteer for Combined Operations, it was perfectly natural that, from a desk at 1A Richmond Terrace, off Whitehall, the Chief of Combined Operations (CCO) should settle his fate. Although, perhaps, it was more of a coincidence that Charles Herlofson's should also be affected, even though he too was about to enter the business of raiding the enemy coastline. But, ironically, while Godwin and Herlofson were enthusiastic about hitting the enemy, CCO himself, the splendidly titled Vice Admiral, Lieutenant General, Air Marshal Lord Louis Mountbatten, was constantly being prevailed upon to deny them that opportunity. The letter before him on the evening of 26 August 1942 was simply the latest attempt by opponents, as well as in this instance, well-meaning friends, to subvert him from the orders of Prime Minister and Chiefs of Staff to carry the war to the enemy. As long ago as May, they had instructed him to mount raids upon the enemy coast to take some of the strain off the hard-pressed Russians who, for a year, had been resisting a German onslaught which still threatened to engulf their country. But as this letter from Vice Admiral Sir Bertram Ramsay suggested, 'perhaps the Chiefs were mistaken', and implied moreover, that he, the man who had saved the British Expeditionary Force from capture at Dunkirk in 1940 and now was designated commander of the naval forces to carry them back into Europe, had a strong vested interest in seeking a reappraisal.

'My dear Dickie', it began. 'Raids on the occupied coast have not done very well in the last 12 months', and subtly pointed out that those which had been made, such as, without naming them, the attack on St. Nazaire in March and the debacle at Dieppe less than a fortnight before, had clearly indicated to the Germans the nature of their weaknesses in defence, making it all the more difficult in the future to launch an attack in force upon the enemy.

Mountbatten's reply was studiously polite but uncompromisingly dismissive, that of a leader who had endured a weary day at meetings and had just

12

settled a pressing family problem before catching up with arrears of less important correspondence. His letter stated an insistence upon the carrying out of imperative orders to raid the enemy intensively as the overture to a major descent to be made on Europe in 1943. And it reflected, to his mounting frustration as he had expressed it recently to a colleague, 'every time I make a suggestion, there are people in the Admiralty who try to squash it'.

It rather seems, in fact, as if Ramsay's letter, in all its mildness, spurred Mountbatten into launching his own furious offensive, not only against the Germans but also his opponents in the other Services, chief among them his own, the Royal Navy. The files for September are full of reports about frequent small raids on the French coast by an organisation called the Small Scale Raiding Force (SSRF) and of papers aimed at eliminating opposition to that force, or any other, doing as CCO pleased. Small-scale raiding had become an issue of faith to Mountbatten, the catalyst of a struggle between the Chiefs of Staff Committee (of which Mountbatten was a member) and Naval Commanders in Chief who conspired frequently to cancel raids at the last moment on the grounds that the value of the objective did not merit the risk of the naval covering force. But of far greater importance than as a means to squash petty intrigue, the prosecution of intensive raiding, as Mountbatten calculated it, was essential to maintain two vital impulses. First, to avoid compromise of the planned Anglo-American landings at three points in Morocco and Algeria, which was intended to turn the existing strategy of defence into one of attack. And second, for the preservation of the enthusiasm of volunteers like Godwin. There is a danger, wrote Mountbatten, that '. . . if small raiding ceased, the enemy's suspicions might be aroused as he came to interpret the large shipping movements associated with the mounting of Operation TORCH'. And as for the chosen raiders in Combined Operations, the anti-climax of inaction against the enemy could only lead to '. . . a progressive decline in discipline and morale . . . the personnel are bound to feel that their services are being wholly wasted'. What they needed was, as he wrote, 'an occasional battle'.

Few in the lower orders who felt frustrated by waiting for something to happen can have understood the nature of the struggles on their behalf which raged above their head and which eventually settled their destiny. Indeed, there were not many combatants for power who can have been aware that the relatively simple issue of to raid or not to raid had its origin, partly, in an authority granted by the Chiefs of Staff to CCO on 27 July to appoint Force Commanders whose task it would be to plan and lead an intensified series of raids of which those by SSRF were but the first. Admirals, of jaundiced eye in particular, interpreted this change of policy to mean that CCO was being granted an autonomy which threatened the sanctity of long-established rights within the military community. They resented a CCO who was getting too big for his boots and who had acquired a 'private' MTB—numbered 344—to sail and raid as he chose in waters which for generations had been controlled by Admiralty. Othello's occupation was threatened.

But CCO was very powerful, of the Blood Royal and much favoured by a Prime Minister who had suffered in the past from the obduracy of Admirals. The small raids continued throughout September, killing Germans almost with impunity, night after night along the enemy coast and only once caught out, and hammered, albeit with the loss of their leader.

Sudden death was an occurrence Mountbatten had come to live with. As commander of a flotilla of destroyers he had lost several ships, including his own, and knew what it was to mourn friends and comrades—and then put the emotion aside and carry on with the war. That was part of the business of high command which got no less painful as he approached a pinnacle and yet kept in touch with those on the lower slopes whom he must thrust into peril. Callous he was not. Officers on his staff in those days, who had observed him facing up to the heavy losses of St. Nazaire and Dieppe, would say he abhorred waste but costed it against the attainment, or otherwise, of the aim. If men were doomed to die at his command, it must be to useful effect after everything possible had been done to give them a chance. So he mourned the dead of SSRF in September and, at the beginning of October, submitted a dossier to Winston Churchill of four successful SSRF operations as proof of the feasibility of repeats on a far wider frontage and depth. Also he organised a selling exercise, to present Captain Geoffrey Appleyard, Royal Army Service Corps, to the Prime Minister, to selected Cabinet Ministers and the Chiefs of Staff, to let this dynamic young man describe his latest exploit on 6 October on the island of Sark. He intended to galvanise the Prime Minister with the thrill of youth's inspirational heroism—and to win permission to turn small-scale raiding into something more potent than an exercise in strategic bluff and morale boosting.

Appleyard was a man apart among commando soldiers. A Cambridge graduate of athletic prowess who was once described as 'an intellectual thug' and to whom the war, along with the killing of Germans, was a consuming obsession. But Operation BASALT had developed into something more than a mere reconnaissance of Sark and an attempt to take prisoners. It had become an unintended turning point in the war, of dreadful significance to anybody engaged in commando work or sabotage. Not only did it yield detailed information about the island's defences from the lips of an old lady, propped up in bed talking to her unexpected midnight visitors with their blackened faces, but it produced items from newspapers revealing a German proclamation directing people to forced labour on the mainland. That was the unsullied aspect of a story related by Appleyard to an enthralled Winston Churchill, senior members of the Cabinet and the Chiefs of Staff on 13 October. The ugly side may not have been mentioned except in passing, but it was equally crucial in measure of violence, for it would have told of three prisoners, one of whom made such a noise that it had been necessary to shoot them all for fear of attracting attention on the way to the boats. And how the Germans found their bodies with hands bound, a measure adopted by Appleyard to hamper any efforts they might make to escape.

The maltreatment of prisoners fatally touched a very sensitive nerve attached to the German hierarchy's pontifical objections to breaches of the Rules of War, as the shooting of bound men undoubtedly was. With scandalised indignation and a bland effacement of their own murder and maltreatment of prisoners, they already had protested vigorously about written orders found on Canadian soldiers after the Dieppe raid which authorised the binding of prisoners to hamper the destruction of captured documents. And, ever since amphibious commando raids had started in 1940, it had become the habit of the German Chancellor, Adolf Hitler, to fulminate and classify all raiders, uniformed or not, as *franc-tireurs*—an emotive label in the German military vocabulary dating back to 1870 when *amour propre* had been offended by civilian guerillas making a nuisance of themselves behind the lines. The outrage on Sark stimulated the abiding hatred in Hitler's mind and provided a pretext for the immediate issue of a long contemplated announcement. It contained the gist, but not all the legal ramifications, of what was at once made notorious as 'The Hitler Commando Order':

> 'From October 8 at 12 noon, all British officers and men captured at Dieppe will be put in chains. . . . In future, all sabotage and terror tactics by the British and their accomplices, who behave like bandits rather than soldiers, will be treated as such by German troops and will be ruthlessly exterminated wherever they appear.'

Churchill, at Mountbatten's request, had retaliated already by having numbers of German troops manacled, in the confident assurance that there now were enough German prisoners in British hands to compel second thoughts by the other side—as, in due course, happened. As everybody felt at the time, it was an uncomfortable business, as much against the grain as had been Appleyard's split second decision (which saddened him) to kill the recalcitrant prisoners. Yet these were the inevitable outgrowths of the sabotage and guerilla warfare upon which commandos were embarked, another facet of the insidiously mounting clandestine warfare being fermented throughout a German Reich in which the still more insidious Nazi apparatus held stronger sway than ever. In this atmosphere, Appleyard could inspire his audience with the cleaner side of his adventure story and Mountbatten could capitalise on a shrewd sales exercise by obtaining the permission he sought to extend small-scale raiding. Thereupon it was simply a matter of advertising throughout the Ministries and agencies in search of suggestions for suitable targets and start the recruitment of more dedicated young men of the Appleyard stamp for whom the war was a personal matter.

Casting about for ideas, Mountbatten's staff at Richmond Terrace fastened at once upon seaboards which had long been used by raiders and secret agents—the long, heavily indented and island dotted coastlines of Brittany and, most strategically lucrative of all, of Norway. As ever, the economists were anxious to stop movement of iron ore from Narvik through the Inner Leads to the steel-making plants of Germany. Warships and aircraft had frequently tried without lasting effect. Occasional raids by the highly trained volunteer Commando forces to destroy enemy installations and shipping and, perhaps, bring out Norwegians to whom freedom was vital, had done as much harm as good. For the reprisals stirred up by the raids—the putting of homes to the torch and the removal of men folk to Grini and the other concentration camps springing up all over the country and throughout Europe—was counter-productive of future resistance. Anxiously, King Haakon, his government and General Hansteen, the Norwegian Commander-in-Chief, fretted over the harm being done to the people's will at no great cost to the Germans who, after each raid, frequently gave another twist to the screw of repression.

It was, of course, far easier for the British to justify their activities on the grounds that war was war, implying the Norwegians must suffer in silence. Yet it was prospective Norwegian involvement in the raiding of the Inner Leads which presented Mountbatten with the opening he sought, the coming to his notice, through Admiralty channels, of Operations codenamed VP which were to be executed by the 30th Norwegian Motor Torpedo Boat Flotilla (of which Charles Herlofson's MTB was a part) once the hours of darkness permitted towards the end of October.

As an artist in bending other people's concepts to his own designs, Mountbatten deftly, and with a charm cultivated to shift mountains of obduracy, merged VP operations with commando raids. Gently the naval planners at the Admiralty were seduced to appreciate the undoubted advantages of landing commando parties from MTBs to seize the German light defensive positions in the narrow entrances to fjords and thus enable the MTBs right of entry to attack the shipping within. With slick efficiency, the planners were presented with a comprehensive list, along with precise details of targets, all as part of what Combined Operations codenamed Operation OMNIBUS. Taking it a step farther, Mountbatten then expressed his fears that there might be a clash between operations schemed by separate, unco-ordinated agencies, 'of which I have had recent experience elsewhere'. And would it not be desirable for the joint VP and OMNIBUS business to be dealt with by his headquarters, acting in concert with the Whitehall ministries and the Admiral Commanding Orkneys and Shetland (ACOS), who was the authority for all operations against the Norwegian coast and under whom 30th Flotilla came? Swiftly and painlessly it was done. The Chiefs of Staff approved. Thereupon it was only necessary to work out procedures and create the commando forces required to carry out their minor depredations while the MTBs got on with the more solid business of mining the waterways and torpedoing ships.

The speed at which Mountbatten put together the OMNIBUS package has rarely been commented upon and was completed barely in time. The organisation he had refined since taking over little more than a year ago was designed for quick reaction, although at this moment none too well supplied with all the necessary forces. Only one Commando, No. 12, was immediately ready for small-scale raiding, the others having either been used up elsewhere or being committed already to TORCH. Fortunately 12 Commando was ideal for the job. All along it had specialised in smaller raids and had provided a few of its brightest staff to the SSRF. In a way it had about it the talents, attitude and aura which in later days would be associated with the Special Air Service. So it was natural for Mountbatten to look there for an officer as Force Commander and to find one Captain F. W. (Ted) Fynn, a Gordon Highlander who had come up from the ranks and personified all that was best in that combative regiment, allied to an independence of mind which in peacetime might not necessarily have matched smoothly with the social graces of an illustrious regular battalion's officers' mess. Nobody seems to have paid much attention to the title of what later would become known as North Force. For the time being it was called Fynn Force, which suited the 65 officers and men from D Troop of 12 Commando under Fynn's command, since it was their leader, as a man of sense, nerve and drive, who mattered more than a title. And these were the attributes which the ten Norwegian members of No. 10 (Inter-Allied) Commando came to like when they too moved north to play an essential part in winter warfare in their own country.

Needless to say, neither 10 nor 12 Commando could provide all the specialists needed to paddle canoes in the fjords or ski across a snow-capped hinterland. Only a few like Lieutenant Ken Waggett, The Middlesex Regiment, knew how to canoe; or like Sergeant Jack Cox, Somerset Light Infantry, had learnt to ski. It was Mountbatten who, for security and urgency, by-passed the normal channels to raise a brand new Commando—No. 14—the job of his staff at Combined Operations HQ (COHQ) to assemble a rare mixture of canoists and skiers recruited from Army and Navy, Canadians and British, to fill its *ad hoc* establishment. It was all completed with incredible speed, just as the electrifying news of the TORCH landings in North Africa broke. Suddenly an end to the war came into sight. Somewhat unexpectedly perhaps, Lieutenant Colonel E. A. M. Wedderburn, the Royal Scots, found himself officially Commander of 14 (Arctic) Commando on 11 November and already in close touch with the two officers who were to be his Troop Commanders. Four days later one of these, Lieutenant A. Courtauld, RNVR, presented himself at HMS *Dorlin* at Acharacle on the west coast of Scotland to pick one officer, one petty officer and fifteen ordinary seamen from among the élite Royal Navy small boatmen and canoists assembled there. Competition was fierce, but from the short list there emerged men whose calibre and skills seemed outstanding— John Godwin, Petty Officer Harold Hiscock and Ordinary Seamen Keith Mayor, Andrew West and Neville Burgess. Now Godwin's saga would begin in earnest.

4

Back to the Fjords

When John Godwin reported to HMS *Northney* at Hayling Island, between Portsmouth and Chichester, it was to find himself in a metropolis of amphibious activity where the talk was all of small boats and craft, and the intentions entirely aggressive. In that rather bleak spot, located not too far from lively flesh pots which included London, he was to rub shoulders with those dedicated to the mission of one day landing armies on the enemy coast as the first step in bringing the war to an end. At *Northney* the sailors belonging to Combined Operations received their initial training in watermanship, rudimentary navigation and weaponry and were introduced to the vessels in which they were to serve—mechanised ramped landing craft (LCMs); ramped, wooden assault craft (LCAs) with a speed up to 10 knots; even faster Higgins Eureka craft known as Landing Craft Personnel (LCPs); plus dozens of other types of strange shape and with odd variations. It was the world of the small boat enthusiast devilling in waters which had long been a mecca for their kind, a wartime capitalisation on yachtsmen's peacetime pursuits. Also the home of private armies with peculiar craft which were only whispered about in the close circles to which they belonged: shadowy groups of tight-lipped men with desperate missions in mind and misleading titles such as Party Inhuman, Combined Operations Pilotage Party (COPP) or Royal Marine Boom Patrol Detachment (RMBPD) whose craft was usually the canoe.

Once Godwin had assimilated the basic lessons of boat handling on treacherous beaches in competition with tide, current and the ever-threatening vicissitudes of changing wind, visibility, darkness and phosphorescence in a fast craft's wake, he too turned to canoes. He had heard of how a submarine's officer had first put forward in the summer of 1940 an idea about the potential of the collapsible Folbot canoe, then being issued to submarines, as suitable for carrying raiders inshore and, almost unobserved, attacking ships at anchor. He gathered this idea had been seized upon by Mountbatten's predecessor, Admiral of the Fleet Sir Roger Keyes, and given to the Commandos to develop for a special raiding role, and how in several daring missions they had reconnoitred beaches along with RN officers, and sunk ships. Further inquiries revealed the existence of all sorts of collapsible, lightweight boats, each suited to a specific task. Goatley dories, for example, which SSRF had often used to carry them to and from MTB 344; and the Goatley Cockleshell canoes with which RMBPD was later to win immortality as the 'Cockleshell Heroes'. Canoes, to Godwin, assumed the guise of a knight's charger, a rapier in Combined Operation's armoury which promised, so he thought, to help him mount a personal assault upon the enemy.

They sent him to HMS *Dorlin* in Scotland to work with special craft. There he mastered many new skills and also, by permission of a laird, indulged in an earlier and much loved pursuit of fishing for salmon and sea trout in excellent waters. He rarely did anything by half-measures, and here he impressed his superiors with a dedication at work and play. Quite naturally he was high on the list of those chosen for the most exacting tasks or forlorn hopes.

It was Lieutenant Courtauld's problem on 15 November 1942 to make just such a choice, to pick sixteen men from many applicants in a single day for a new type of mission in Arctic waters. There is a consensus among those who knew Godwin which says he often gave a poor impression at first acquaintance. 'Quite undistinguished except for a quiet readiness to do what his superior told him', thought Professor M. R. D. Foot, in retrospect, who once briefed him for an operation. 'Eccentric—dress liable to turn an RN officer purple—hesitant with senior officers—diffident—stood back—unambitious', thought Ken Waggett who got to know him well. Clearly none of these deficiencies, if deficiencies they were in a man of action, would worry Courtauld during their meeting. He had read the reports of Godwin's instructors. No doubt he sensed the responsible enthusiasm of this slim young man. Possibly there was an instant rapport between them, transmitted on the narrow beam of Godwin's charisma (deny it as one might) which was the opposite of charisma as broadcast on all frequencies, for example, by Mountbatten to reach every corner of a room and influence the most insensitive person present. Be that as it may, within the space of a working day one Sub-Lieutenant RNVR and sixteen companions, among them Godwin's own chosen 'gang', were heading south on fourteen unexpected days' leave with an undisclosed but guaranteed perilous task looming ahead.

Even as Godwin and his men were at home, trying to keep absolutely to themselves the secrets of their task, their leaders were formulating plans and assembling forces. Already the 30th MTB Flotilla was installed at Lerwick and coming to grips with life in a lively community with its own peculiar diversions amid the divisions of war. They were not the only Norwegians thereabout; a few miles distant, at Sullom Voe, there harboured a small rugged group of seamen, outcasts from the fjords and secretively engaged in plying to and from home waters carrying agents and escapers. They were the conductors of the celebrated Shetland Bus who, off duty, sometimes came to Lerwick, to relax and, perhaps, to do battle with their smartly attired countrymen of the Royal Norwegian Navy (RNN)—partly for the sheer hell of it, partly over the local women—although Charles Herlofson was at a loss to understand why, since, as far as he could see, the 'best' had left for the mainland and those who remained were hard at work knitting sweaters for record wages of £20 or more a week. All was turmoil on Saturday nights, as soldiers of the garrison and airmen from the airfield came into town, these lowly paid British with only a few pounds in their pockets. At times, amid the rutting, it was difficult to believe they were all on the same side against Germany.

Fortunately the war obtruded for the rest of the time when Vice Admiral Lionel Wells, in his appointment as ACOS at Lyness, Orkney, kept them all on the go, forging ahead with militant projects which were complementary to VPs and OMNIBUS. Wedderburn came to examine accommodation for his men and look at training areas. Ted Fynn arrived mid-November, his mind open to plans already under consideration by CCO and ACOS, but primarily intent upon going across to Norway to study the battleground for himself. At 0815 hours, Sunday 22 November, he embarked as a spectator of a VP operation at the Sogne Sea and at once experienced the rough side of travelling in one among a group of three of these fast boats.

The Fairmile 'D' Class MTB was a hybrid, a clever splicing by the Royal Corps of Naval Constructors of a destroyer-type bow to a fast motor boat stern which engineered a heavily armed 95-foot craft with quite remarkably good seakeeping characteristics and a top speed of around 30 knots. They were ideal for turbulent Norwegian waters where only the most extraordinary conditions could overwhelm them. But as Ted Fynn soon discovered, comfort was not among their best attributes. Once under way in a force 6 wind, spray would begin to break over the bows, soaking all on deck and causing the two other groups to turn back. Herlofson's system, as with the other skippers, was to have only four men above deck except when at action stations, the rest staying below, trying to keep dry and warm by paraffin stoves and from the hot food sent up from the electrically heated galley. Those on the bridge were permanently wet, the driving sea penetrating the minutest gap in oil skins and seeping down collars despite plugging holes with towels. Of course, life would be made easier by throttling back the 5000 hp, four-shaft Packard petrol engines, but that might have put an end to life altogether. For the 350-mile journey had to be made to a very discrete schedule, timed precisely to be more than 60 miles out from the enemy coast in daylight to avoid the deadly attention of low-flying fighter aircraft. This was the only airborne threat the MTB men really feared, their single 2-pounder pom-pom gun being no match for it. High speed was therefore often imperative—but quite the opposite once close inshore and within sight of well-known features after navigation ceased to be by dead reckoning and local knowledge became priceless. At this stage experienced officers like Herlofson or ex-merchant seamen and fishermen, who knew the water intimately, took charge, especially because the Germans had long since extinguished all but the land light beacons of the Inner Leads.

Eagerly Fynn soaked up techniques to pass on to his men. Twelve hours after departure, he noted an exact landfall with confirmation by a flare dropped from an RAF aircraft. Then an excrutiating experience, frequently inflicted upon sailors by peculiarities of wind and tide off this stretch of coast; a vortex of lashed water about an hour before entering the fjord '. . . which took the fight out of most of us' — and effectively belied the assertion of some RNN crews that only commandos fouled their boats by being seasick. As suddenly, they were in calm waters and as quickly '. . . all the men were in excellent form'. Now they could proceed at speed, lit by a moon so bright that it was felt too risky to continue until the sky clouded over, since they would have to pass fairly near the very watch posts and batteries which, in due course, would be objectives for Fynn's force. For a couple of hours they tied up under the shadow of some overhanging rocks before trying again to enter the main channel of the principal waterway. At once Fynn was to witness the cat and mouse theme of VPs — a challenge flashed from an enemy patrol boat two miles off, which was in no way satisfied by 'phoney' signals in reply and 'circling round about'. Intrigued, he watched the senior officer making up his mind to refrain from attack, since 'the noise would probably bring the local batteries to bear' and 'a patrol boat was not worth the powder and shot and the confusion it would cause'.

That was the end of it. It was a disappointed and yet pleased Fynn who sat down on the MTB on 24 November to write his report. But already he had enough material for Major Ian Collins at COHQ to fundamentally shape Godwin's saga, and many another man's too.

> 'I am satisfied one could land a number of men and leave them concealed for a couple of weeks. . . . I suggest the Canadian type [canoe] as being more robust and able to carry greater loads. Two or three men could slip into a harbour with a load of limpets unobserved where a D boat could not. . . . Everyone is fit and dying for another crack as soon as the weather improves. I am sure there are infinite possibilities in this game.'

Two days later, as OC troops, he was on board MTB 626, commanded by Lieutenant Knut Bøgeberg, RNN, heading for Nylede in company with four other MTBs split into three groups. This time there was never a dull moment. Two MTBs at once crept into Askevold harbour and, to the delight of commandos and, particularly, the sailors, sank two ships and made off for home after little more than two hours in enemy waters. This, to the delighted MTB captains, was what they were in business for — to see their fish run true, thrill to the flash of impact, and rejoice as the boom of the explosion echoed round harbours and off fjord walls. Then turn tail and scoot for safety before an awakened foe began lacing the air with wild tracer streams in the darkness. Lying up they viewed as an unavoidable ploy to enable the culminating torpedo strike; but the presence of commandos was greeted sceptically. The soldiers cluttered up an already crowded boat, sleeping in gangways and, at times, strained natural patience with their seasickness and demands. A lot of this was nautical conservatism at work, a suspicious resistance to the unorthodox. At first they grudgingly admitted to a certain logic, but utility had to be proved. That was what the other groups were trying to do conclusively this time out.

The second group certainly helped, spending two nights in hiding near Florøland, putting two parties ashore to patrol inland without being spotted. That proved something to Fynn as well. As also did the phenomenon of the fishermen's behaviour at MTB 626's hiding place when, soon after daybreak, they put in their appearance to attend nets and lobster pots. At once they observed a change in the landscape and spotted the well-camouflaged MTBs. Those of insatiable curiosity would stop, scan carefully, and then row across; the prudent would look the other way and keep moving until intercepted by a boat from the MTB and pulled in for interrogation. Fynn believed 'All the fishermen thought at first we were a German Navy Party and refused to discuss politics at all, but after being convinced on board that we were the Allied Forces, gave us a good deal of valuable information.' The bold also helped, at considerable risk, with reconnaissance; one skipper going the whole hog by loaning his boat to take a party into the harbour of Rubbestadnes to attack two enemy boats in the small hours of Sunday—a plan which had to be abandoned due to a typically sudden deterioration of weather.

The game most certainly was on, with Fynn enthusiastic about 'lying up' by MTBs, but also keen on a separate scheme, excluded from OMNIBUS, called COBBLESTONES, which was well favoured by ACOS, who possessed a couple of the 50-foot Norwegian fishing boats of the kind which served the Shetland Bus. Why not use these as carriers of 14 Commando's canoe parties, ACOS had suggested? Let them insert the canoes, for anything up to a fortnight, on small, deserted islands as bases for paddling unnoticed into nearby harbours to fix limpets to the ships at anchor. Why not, indeed, agreed the planners at COHQ. That would be ideal for No. 1 Troop of 14 Commando, once it was trained, leaving 10 and 12 Commandos to support VPs. Thus it was that when Godwin and the others reported back from leave on 29 November they were at once set in motion, Godwin spending four days at Arisaig, learning about the latest limpet mines and explosive techniques, the rest attending a course on the Klepper canoes at the Marshall Street swimming baths in London. Rapidly the pieces were fitted together under the urging of a CCO and staff who desired action soon in order to gain maximum use of the long winter nights before the March equinox made penetration of Norwegian waters impossibly perilous.

Yet already the task was running into difficulty. Urgently the Germans were reviewing measures against a whole series of recent damaging raids—including the blowing up by commandos of a power station at Glomfjord in September, along with minor sabotage by agents; and, of course, the prowling MTBs which were seriously disrupting the vital coastal traffic. Simultaneously in London, the forces of reaction, already so familiar to Mountbatten as squashers of his enterprises, were conspiring, with convincing arguments, to crab his latest initiatives.

5

To Raid
or Not to Raid

By comparison with the political ramifications bearing upon amphibious raiding, the complexities of the actual military operations were simplicity itself, the strains upon the raiders themselves shorter lived than the fears gnawing at the hearts and guts of exiled governments. Few governments agonised more over the by-products of raiding's violence than the Norwegian one. Divorced from their people by over 350 miles of sea, they could but feel their opinions from reports and from a few people recently escaped to Britain. They were denied the opportunities, enjoyed by men like Fynn, Herlofson and Bøgeberg, to actually meet the people on their own doorsteps, so to speak, and judge for themselves the political drift of sentiment. They could only guess at strength of dread, inhibitions and the ancient, hide-bound, Viking bloody-mindedness of a divided populace whose patience was beginning to wear thin, not only with the Royalist and Quisling factions, but also at the profiteers and those who sat apathetically on the fence. It was an instinctive appreciation of the indefinable horrors which might be released if that bloody-mindedness got out of hand which, among other factors, made the king and his ministers baulk at vigorous direct action against the Germans.

From the now widespread network of agents which reported direct by radio or despatch with an expanding organisation across the frontier in Sweden, came evidence of new edicts, ferocious punitive measures and the execution of patriots and saboteurs. Within only a few days of the successful attack on the Glomfjord power station in September and, in December, of an ill-fated attempt to land soldiers to attack the heavy-water plant at Rjukan, the liquidation of those captured was reported by the Norwegian Military Attaché in Stockholm. Simultaneously, by parallel routes, arrived intelligence of an internal political situation in flux. Once more Reich Commissioner Terboven was endeavouring to impose government by Quisling's Najional Samlings Party (the NS), concurrent with gestures of pacifism signalled by the release from prison of detainees whose crime had been their objection to the German presence or the stigma of being Jewish, Communists, an intellectual, or just close friends with the Royal Family. It was known that a few thousand young men had volunteered to fight against Communism in Russia and that members of the NS with nothing now to lose were more ready than ever to inform upon patriots, agents and raiders. These were the by-products of desperation allied with fear of the incoming tide of Allied victories in North Africa and the mighty Russian blow, early in December, cutting off the Germans at Stalingrad. Fence-squatters were reconsidering their position and faint-hearted collaborators, as the saying went, starting to 'row' in the opposite direction. Cautiously, the government in London sometimes pleaded with their British opposite numbers to let the trend alone contribute the main weight of resistance. They feared that the retribution stirred up by pin-prick attacks of slight strategic purpose might undo, at awful suffering for the innocent, the good being done by German and Quisling insensitivity. This was the perpetual dilemma which prompted a pragmatic solicitude to postpone armed action 'until the time was ripe'. Unfortunately, nobody could precisely define when that might be.

General Hansteen, the Norwegian C-in-C, continued with a long running series of objections to commando landings when he heard of COBBLESTONES. The employment of fishing boats and their connection with sabotage must provoke the Germans into taking reprisals against innocent fishermen and, indirectly, cause immense damage to the industry which was contributing most to an already severely rationed diet. That would be counterproductive in every way—economically, physically and psychologically. His arguments carried weight and persuasion. Although the exact sequence of cause and effect of the abandonment of the COBBLESTONE plan are not precisely known, it is apparent that, from the outset, common sense as well as sympathy would lead to acceptance of the Norwegian case and cancellation of the scheme. And this step was made all the more inevitable when, shortly prior to the New Year, the latest German proclamation (posted in the wheelhouse of fishing boats) made it a penal offence NOT to give information about Allied parties and agents. So insidious a measure put the most dedicated patriot, let alone the unstable minority, under the most subtle strain. To the existing impulsion of betrayal for reward was added coercion by fear of omission.

Embargoes are often the incentive of invention, and the evidence is clear that, long before COBBLESTONES were cancelled, the officers of ACOS and 14 Commando were seeking a legal substitute for fishing boats—looking for a military boat of a design which might pass examination as of Norwegian origin. Again, it is not exactly clear who conjured up the idea of adopting the unlikely sounding LCP(M) (Landing Craft Personnel (Medium)) for the task, although judging by the fervour with which Godwin was to sponsor its use, we may assume it was he who started it. It is, of course, just possible that a pun upon COBBLESTONES gave a lead to consideration of the LCP(M), the design of which was based on that of the Northumberland coble, and a fact that it was nearly always referred to as 'the coble'. But almost anybody involved in training at HMS *Dorlin* would have been aware of how well this heavy, 39-foot × 10-foot wooden, clinker-built craft with twin lifting rudders could work in rough waters off exposed and rocky shores. Powered by a 65 hp Scripps Ford V8 petrol engine, it might not only be expected to perform satisfactorily in Norwegian waters and perhaps be taken for a locally built craft, it could carry up to 20 men or, more to the requirement, two Klepper canoes.

Differences of opinion there would be over the LCP(M)'s virtues, but many were set at rest when Lieutenant Courtauld sailed one from Fort William to the Shetlands on 28 December to present her, along with criticism for a tendency to ship water in heavy seas. Five days later, Hogmanay intervening, Fynn was asking Lieutenant A. Job, RNVR, the Operations Staff Officer who liaised between Fynn Force and 30th Flotilla, for 'two cobles'. And at once it was Godwin who took a close interest in this craft and began devising ways of stowing canoes aboard it as well as turning over means of employing this combination of assault craft.

Precise entries in official diaries and postwar comments by those involved transmit a clear impression of unusually erratic evolution of Fynn Force's approach to battle. Allowing that amphibious raiding was invariably the prey to the fluctuations of vacillation and internal factors, it does appear that Fynn's party received more than its due share of amendments. For one thing, the various elements of the force were never concentrated in one place but remained spread throughout Scotland and the Shetlands. Also it was a long time settling down to uninterrupted training, No. 1 Troop canoists suffering more than the skiers of No. 2 from an excess of itinerancy. For no sooner had Godwin and the others arrived in mid-December, and by dribs and drabs by destroyer, at Balta, on the islet of Unst, than it became plain that the local waters were so storm wracked as to be almost useless for continuous practice. As a result it was decided by Wedderburn on Christmas Day that they should return to Scotland in the New Year and set up shop at Loch Carron—a change of location which was delayed for three boring weeks during which Godwin's fascination with the coble was allowed to flourish.

Over Christmas Mountbatten also became aware of yet another and more powerful attempt to curtail raiding than that already posed by the Norwegians. To begin with, it came from a most august personage, none other than the mysterious 'C', Head of the SIS (Secret Intelligence Service), Major General Sir Stewart Menzies. SIS was in a pinch, its jealously guarded function as the main provider of information to the British government and Services only recently recovering from the loss of its principal agents and networks in Europe in 1939 and 1940. 'C' was also disturbed (to put it mildly) by powerful rivals who had entered the arena at the nadir of his fortunes—namely the exiled governments in London and, more aggravating, local interlopers such as SOE and COHQ, all of whom had their foreign contacts. The burden of Menzies's current protest lay in the assertion that raiding by SOE and COHQ in Brittany and Norway was endangering the insertion and picking up of agents from those relatively safe and quiescent beaches. His keenest ally was by nature the Director of Naval Intelligence who, in collaboration with other disaffected deities in Admiralty, recognised a wonderful opportunity to clip the wings of the interlopers—principally SOE. Learned papers were composed and influential lobbies sounded. At a meeting of the Chiefs of Staff Committee on 4 January, Mountbatten and SOE (who were not present) were told that future raids in the two sensitive areas must be approved first by 'C'—creating what became known at Richmond Terrace as the C Ban. As it turned out, the ban was not nearly so prohibitive of operations against Norway as it was against those in Brittany, which were almost wiped out. But not for love of COHQ as for naval glory. Admiralty and SIS turned a self-interested blind eye to nearly anything associated with tackling enemy shipping. Indeed, at the same meeting which applied the C Ban, another attempt by General Hansteen to restrict operations in Norway, due to the latest German threat of death for those who did not report saboteurs, was set aside. The Chiefs of Staff gave the subject a good airing and admitted it was a matter of the highest political importance—but declined to admit to an 'escape clause' by which the Norwegians might permit raiding against their country 'subject to restrictions'. In plain terms, Mountbatten was told that nothing was intended to limit any proposals for attacks on land targets. And with that Mountbatten must have been fairly content, particularly since he had retained the right of appeal if 'C' and Admiralty employed the C Ban too strictly.

For immediately afterwards 'C' agreed a number of targets permissible for attack, and on 5 January Mountbatten sent the Outline Plan for OMNIBUS to ACOS, requesting that he arrange for it to be mounted. The impression, however, that all barriers had been removed and that raiding would be as intense as 'C' allowed was absent. Both in Mountbatten's letter to ACOS (Vice-Admiral Wells) and within the Outline Plan, doubts prevailed and flexibility was rife. Mountbatten admitted that 'I do not think it will often be possible to decide on the actual objectives to be attacked, when the force sails, and this will on your instructions have to be left to the discretion of the Naval and Military Force Commanders.' That, he thought, would be 'quite practical, as the military forces will be fully briefed with intelligence and plans of objectives in the area'. But wide latitude, as many experienced raiders might fear, could lead to all sorts of local improvisations and, perhaps, with irony, attacks on targets precluded by 'C'. A note of uncertainty sounded on the subject of associated raids, including CARTOON, which Fynn Force was already planning against Stord Island later in the month—'If the above operations are proceeded with', said the Outline Plan.

Doubts from above percolated below. Enterprising junior officers involved with a winter war in the fjords, which was slow maturing, began to formulate plans of their own. Boredom had its say. Morale demanded a sense of purpose. Living conditions in huts were rough at Sullom Voe; water had to be boiled before drinking, transport limited to a couple of motor cycles, a pick-up and one 3-ton truck; communications by a single telephone line; women in short supply and leave at a premium.

6

The CARTOON Effect

Godwin and the canoeists were living in comfort at the Loch Carron Hotel and training hard around the loch, when word of Operation CARTOON filtered through at the end of January. MTB crews and Commandos had taken casualties, it was said. But before they could reduce rumours to solid facts, orders arrived telling Godwin to pick four companions and shift to Lerwick at once. Hearts gave a jump, stomachs turned over as imaginations raced. Yet not a moment too soon was the routine of training, training and more training and monotony replaced by a run for goal. But where and how? COBBLESTONES, Godwin knew, had been abandoned. Was this his moment, an opportunity to try out the coble?

There was an overall feeling of unsuppressed excitement in the air when they arrived at Lerwick on 3 February. To the supreme news from Russia of the surrender at Stalingrad of the German Sixth Army and of electrifying successes in North Africa was added the thrill of the CARTOON story which had generated so much enthusiasm in the Shetlands. The raid had fulfilled promise, answered questions and provoked invention. It had been, as told by Fynn and others, 'an in and out job' with no lying up or lurking. Four MTBs packed with 53 members of 12 Commando and a detachment of Norwegians from 10 Commando had as their target the pyrite mines on the island of Stord between Bergen and Stavanger. A covering force of three MTBs, one of them Herlofson's 619, had carried out a VP operation, darting into the nearby Liervik harbour after enemy shipping. The long night of 23/24 January had been one gigantic firework display. Despite drawing a blank at Liervik, the covering force soon caught a 2,000-ton ship, raked it with gunfire and set it ablaze as it ran ashore. It engaged too in a brisk exchange with enemy guns, the tracer criss-crossing in brilliant fury, doing little harm but distracting attention from the imbroglio at Sägvag, just around the headland. Here, half the force swept alongside the quay, guns blazing at the four known, but unoccupied, gun positions. Instead, a rattle of small arms fire lashed back from a surprised garrison, which, with ruthless efficiency, was hunted down, killed or captured, one terrified German being chased bare footed along a railway track. Across the bay, the other half force had landed in a small cove and set off for Lillebo at the trot, each man carrying 50 lb of explosives besides his weapons. Two miles and 25 minutes later they were in possession of the mine; three hours later back at Sägvag, leaving the mine a flaming wreck, winding gear and plant shattered beyond repair for up to a year. Withdrawal too had been dramatically executed to the concussion of exploding gun positions and ammunition dumps and a final blow by the covering force MTB, when they were attacked by aircraft and managed to shoot down a bomber.

'Your turn next', Fynn told Godwin with infective glee. 'The Chief and ACOS have had their heads together and that's why you are here.'

When the two Vice Admirals had met in the immediate aftermath of CARTOON it had been in aggressive mood tempered by sympathetic endeavour to reach common ground from different directions. With light resources they strove to strike heavy blows, Mountbatten willingly agreeing that the Admiralty's desire to sink shipping with torpedo and mine from MTBs had first priority; ACOS seeking ways to ease the passage of the MTBs into the harbours and fjords where the ships sheltered behind the coastal defences. 'That is', he pointed out, 'they might get in by surprise but not out unless your commandos land prior to the MTBs entrance and engaged the gun posts while the MTBs withdrew.' This was risky, but Mountbatten was prepared to hazard the commandos and also to encourage a suggestion by his Major Collins that parties of two or three military personnel should be put ashore during darkness so as to be able to report to the MTBs as to whether enemy shipping was in a particular fjord or not. And Collins had also won approval for the idea that canoeists dropped by MTBs about 400 to 800 yards from a fjord's entrance might be able to go in to attack shipping with limpets. Vice Admiral Wells had liked that, the one idea which had led to Godwin coming to Lerwick to be placed under command of Fynn—whose promotion to Major had just come through. Together the two Admirals and their staff officers schemed, pondering what the enemy might do in reply and how to keep one step ahead in the cat and mouse game; seeking ways to improve intelligence about the enemy. Planning, even, to turn sailors into soldiers of a sort by teaching them how to operate their own shore parties, thus moving towards the next operation called CRACKERS.

In addition to the reinforcements from No. 14 Commando, Fynn had also acquired from No. 12 another officer of special accomplishments. Lieutenant Kenyon Waggett was rather more than in the classic cast of the tough, resourceful and thinking infantryman required of the best commando officers who pre-war had learnt to canoe. He was, of two years' standing a Battle School Instructor, imbued with a killer's instinct and latest methods which had exempted him from the normal commando course at Achnaccary. A picked man, well qualified for the role Fynn had in mind for him as Force Commander of small raids to come, such as CRACKERS. A friendly, understanding person too, who was likely to understandingly weld together diverse mixtures of fighting men such as MTB commanders, like Charles Herlofson, and Army, Navy and Norwegian commandos.

In Waggett, Godwin found the mentor he badly needed, somebody a year younger than himself in whom he could confide without being rebuffed; whose willingness to give careful consideration even to the wildest scheme disarmed Godwin's impatient resentment of criticism. Just the man with whom to discuss his pet coble scheme. The plan was a simple interpolation of the original COBBLESTONES fishing boat operation alloyed with VPs. Stow two Klepper canoes, their crews, stores and weapons into the coble; tow it by MTB across the North Sea and slip the tow within a few miles of the coast (letting the MTB return to Lerwick); lurk on a deserted island overlooking some busy anchorage and attack shipping with limpets. Then, after a fortnight's hide-and-seek with the Germans (and the Norwegian police and Quislings, no doubt), rendezvous with the MTB and come home. To Waggett the prospects of success for so imaginative a scheme seemed reasonably good, providing certain technical problems could be resolved, and granted that modicum of luck which all such ventures demand. Listening to John Godwin expounding, he was struck by an enthusiasm which, he felt, excluded self-interest and contained an analytical consideration of the pros and cons along with anxiety to hear suggestions before taking his idea to Fynn and those above. Knowing that they were both soon to embark with Klepper canoes on Operation CRACKERS, Waggett reasoned that the suitability of these craft in Norwegian waters might be tested in conjunction with an examination of Godwin and his men, and prior to that examining the basic feasibility of loading the coble with canoes and finding out how this combination performed when under high-speed tow by an MTB.

Playing around with the next plan but one while working up for its immediate predecessor could, by no great stretch of imagination, be rated an unwise deviation from the aim. Perhaps it was for that reason that, when Godwin and Waggett put the coble idea to Fynn (and caught that officer's interest), the subsequent trial, though not cursory, was not all-embracing either. But because Lieutenant Job (reflecting his Admiral's liking for canoe attacks) and Major Collins (backing his own judgement) recognised it as a splendid way of implementing the soaring notions of the recent meetings between Wells and Mountbatten, nothing was put in the way of a stowage and towing trial. Restraints were unwelcome. Doubts about Godwin and his beloved coble, as tentatively expressed by a shrewd and overworked Norwegian officer, Lieutenant Leif Utne, who was Intelligence, Planning and Operations officer for 30th Flotilla, were brushed aside. To begin with, Utne's feelings were more instinctive than logically argued; simply the coble struck him as an unusual looking craft which, in Norwegian waters, would attract unwanted attention to itself because it was so unlike the locally built boats. But the trials passed muster, as far as they went. That is to say, it was found that there was room enough for two canoes and six or seven men aboard the coble, although a full loading was not attempted. Likewise, the coble towed satisfactorily at speed (with its screws running free from the motor), but only over a short course. After that, the coble was pulled out of the water to allow the satisfied Godwin to join the more pressing business of preparing for CRACKERS.

The two weeks at Loch Carron had put more than polish on Godwin's party's canoeing techniques. In chill waters they had come to appreciate what Eskimos and Arctic explorers, including Roal Amundsen in his North Pole Expedition of 1926, knew. That the collapsible canoe, designed by a Bavarian early in the century, was ideal for their task. Which was hardly surprising in light of the fact that Johann Klepper had based his original design upon the Eskimo kayak which was wider, more capacious and sat lower on the water than the Folbots and Goatley canoes used elsewhere in Combined Operations. Moreover, the Klepper, unlike most other canoes, could be righted by its crew if it capsized, and had an invaluable 'button-up' facility to keep its occupants and contents dry and moderately warm. When it came to operating in Norwegian waters (where Klepper-type canoes were quite common), this could make all the difference to survival under threat of exposure and death from hypothermia.

Team work was of the essence when propelling a two- or three-man canoe at sustained speeds of as much as 3 to 4 knots in reasonably smooth water. But with the slightest 'lop' on the water it was exhausting as well as demanding great skill. A crew wielding double paddles had to work in perfect unison, their pace that of the slowest member, otherwise paddles would clash or interlock — perhaps with fatal consequences. For with loss of power and momentum in turbulent waters, control would be forfeit and an irrecoverable capsize caused. Strength and stamina were at a premium. Much would depend upon the man occupying the centre position of a three-man crew such as Godwin intended to employ. Indeed, he was known as the 'Power House' or 'Engine Room'. The bow position also called for a skilled paddler with keen eyesight, since it was his task also to look out for underwater obstacles which could quite easily rip open a canoe. Usually the leader would sit in the stern, from whence even a whisper could be heard, but which was the best place to command and navigate by map and prismatic compass.

But thrustful paddling in open waters was not the only skill Godwin's men had to master. They had to be able to do it with clean strokes, the minimum disturbance of the water, and no noise when in the presence of the enemy. They had to learn how to close unnoticed upon a ship and fix the magnetic limpet mines to steel sides or, in the case of wooden-hulled vessels, screwed into the timber. And they had also to learn how to operate on land; how to hide among rocks and amidst foliage; how to watch from hidden observation posts without being seen, and how to keep warm and well-fed in some of the most exacting climatic conditions in the world. As sailors, they knew that in Arctic and, at best, even sub-Arctic conditions how death took its toll insidiously of ignorant or careless victims.

On Loch Carron Godwin settled upon who would crew with who and confirmed the suitability and, above all, ingrained determination of the sailors he had selected at HMS *Dorlin*. That they were all volunteers was, of course, a help, and yet no guarantee that they would make the grade in the rigorous days ahead. Volunteers did not always visualise the trials to come and were known to regret! Right from the start the 27-year-old Newfoundlander, Petty Officer Harold (Shorty) Hiscock, stood out as the heart of dependability, an experienced seaman and coxswain who combined professional skills with that fair-minded application of intelligent discipline found in the best senior ratings. Hiscock became second-in-command of the group and, in due course, master of the coble—a most trusted subordinate whose job it would be to stand in for Godwin or act in an independent role if required. They had good men to lead and command, including three young seamen, all in their nineteenth or twentieth years, each from separate parts of the country and trained in different professions. Yet similar in background, motivation and, of vital importance, already experienced in the handling of canoes.

The eldest among them was Andrew West, a house decorator from Glasgow and arguably the strongest among a trio who were more noticeably compact in physique than massive in frame. He, like all the others, of necessity had to be eager to 'do his bit', to be unafraid or, perhaps, unaware of the true danger of a new calling, but proudly intent upon doing something special and avoiding the slightest stigma of being a schrimshanker. Difficult as they might have found it precisely to put into words why they exposed themselves to danger beyond the normal call of duty, they probably would have disclaimed any outstanding patriotic motive—true to their nation's cause, as they were—without making a big song and dance about it. Indeed, only Keith Mayor (along with Godwin as it happened) was prone publicly to enthuse over king and country—and Mayor's background as a factory worker from Preston in Lancashire was perfectly normal, coming as he did from a lower middle-class home—a Boy Scout, well read, regular churchgoer with some knowledge of boats and a distaste for bullies. This really is the point; they were all 'normal' young men faced by a challenge to their manhood, who, as Mayor put it, 'would kill only to prevent themselves from being killed', but whose sense of adventure drove them a little bit farther than some others in the achievement of special standards of performance.

Take, for example, Neville Burgess, the baby of the crew, who had sung in Beverley Minster choir, been a member of the Church Lads Brigade, a very good footballer and a strong swimmer who had left school at 14 and quickly learnt to become a skilled butcher who had no qualms over killing. Involvement with boats, the local shipyard at his home town of Beverley in Yorkshire, the river, the canals and the canoe he shared with a friend, had stimulated his sense of adventure. Until he was old enough to volunteer for the Royal Navy he had contributed to the war effort as best he could — as a motor cycle despatch rider in the Home Guard — before joining HMS *Ganges* at Harwich in June 1942, aged 18. Choice of the Navy was logical, and volunteering for small craft natural. That took him to Inverary in Scotland to learn about Landing Craft Assault, and there, almost inevitably, an old bug bit him again. Within less than a month (in mid-September) he had heard about a call for volunteers for canoeists prepared for special tasks. Little did he know then what he was letting himself in for, although maybe the future looked a trifle more threatening when he arrived at HMS *Dorlin* to discover that among his new comrades were not only youngsters like West and Mayor, from industrial towns, but also Red Indians from the backwoods of Canada.

Godwin chose West as his bowman, leaving Mayor and Burgess to crew together, with the former in command. Paddling, exercising and perspiring in unison and close proximity broke down the traditional dividing lines between officer and man to be found in ships of the Royal Navy. Indeed, of the quartet, Godwin was the only one to have experienced it — on the lower deck — and to him, in any case, the 'regular' RN approach to man management was instinctively foreign. Yet autocratic he could be and conscious of the meaning of the authority vested in the King's Commission, without making it obligatory to stand apart from his followers. If time permitted, he would explain his intentions, while finding nothing incompatible between the function of command and the shared intimacy of leading a private sabotage team. Apparently, air crews and tank crews enjoyed a similar relationship. Why not a canoe crew, shudder as members of the old-school RN might? During those days on Loch Carron, Hiscock, West, Mayor and Burgess allowed themselves to fall completely under Godwin's spell — partly because he willed it and very much because, having voluntarily committed themselves for a dangerous mission, they had little choice but to trust him implicitly. Yet it was the spell which ruled, the charm cast upon them by a leader whose flow of succinctly chosen phrases projected an exhaustive enthusiasm for cobles, canoes, kayaks, explosives and limpets — a magic innoculation with the embodiment of Godwin's own implied infallibility against any doubts they harboured concerning the uncertainties of forthcoming enterprises.

As a close-knit family they had arrived back at Lerwick, apprehensive of their future, confident in their craft (in every sense), anxious to cross the dividing line between training's monotony and action's thrill, eager to put their team spirit to the test. Then, as is so often the way in the military environment, Godwin was told that plans were changing along with the mode of operation. The carefully welded canoe teams, upon which they believed survival depended, were to be disrupted.

'On CARTOON [explained Fynn to a disappointed Godwin] we were about fourteen of our chaps per MTB. Packing them in the aisles, squalid at any time, unmentionable when it got rough. Fourteen hours each way was about all anybody could stand of that, and you could see the sailors had just about enough of it. So for a three day lying up effort like CRACKERS you cannot expect anybody to put up with conditions like that. I've agreed with the Flotilla Leader and with Charles Herlofson, who is leading this time, that eight per boat is the most they can be expected to carry. Now, Ken Waggett wants all the trained assault commandos possible. We also think a couple of Norwegian commandos should go for contact with the locals inland. Even if we take only one two man canoe party, including yourself, that leaves Ken only, himself and nine. Not many. But it will have to do. So, yourself and one other only Jo. Alright?'

It had to be. Fynn was a man who could charm birds out of the trees. Godwin took it quite well and set about repairing the damage. Since canoes were to be employed chiefly for carrying reconnaissance parties, the two Norwegian commandos, Sergeant Bjornsted and Corporal Solum, might have to ride in the canoes. Alright, teach them to paddle. There was not much time, but it would be better than nothing and they were both good-looking types, strong, fit and, as far as could be told, willing to have a go. There was less than three weeks, though.

7

Rough in the Sogne Sea

VPK, CRACKERS or OMNIBUS 42 (call them what you will) were the names embracing the joint ventures ordered by several authorities for probing the mighty Sognefjord. VPK was the next in succession of the Admiralty's sustained attempt to sink shipping by mine and torpedo—carried out this time with Lieutenant Herlofson as Naval Force Commander in MTB 619 and Lieutenant Henrickson's MTB 627 as running companion. CRACKERS and OMNIBUS 42 were COHQ supplements to VPK using Lieutenant Waggett's commandos to assist the MTBs. But as additional, unnamed tasks, there was the picking up of an endangered 'flower' (one of 'C's' agents whose future was in jeopardy from German attention) from the post office at Krakhelle, and the trial of a Klepper canoe by Godwin and Ordinary Seaman West.

They left Lerwick early in the afternoon of 22 February, tested their guns with sharp bursts of fire outside the harbour and headed east in moderate seas. At 0100 hours the entrance to the Krakhellesund was in sight in bright moonlight, and shortly communication established with the 'flower'. This, the initial contact with the shore, was the true start of the operation, the moment at which danger, the fear of entering an enemy trap, began to creep over them. Engines reduced to a low rumble, guns trained and loaded, all hands on deck scanning for trouble, while the skiff's crew paddled for the shore, expressed anxiety followed by relief when the engines opened up the instant the agent came aboard. Up on the bridge Herlofson greeted the agent, a broad smile on his face. The name he had been given might not match that of this passenger, but the face was familiar, that of a comrade of 1940, one of the intrepid Rifle Club which had appointed him as their leader in April 1940, and had since served his king until things had grown too hot nearly three years later.

'I am glad to have you again on my boat and to have been in time.'
'It is kind of you to fetch me. I do not think it would have lasted much longer. There were signs, you know; the Quislings and others. They are always suspicious these days.'

More than that he hardly spoke for the rest of the voyage. Three years of clandestine life taught security lessons the hard way. And even now, the less they said to each other the better, just in case they should yet fall into enemy hands and be played off against each other by astute SD interrogators who rarely missed a trick. The meaning of incarceration in one of the Gestapo houses, in Grini, or the march to the scaffold, had long overshadowed resisters as well as several MTB crew members. Godwin, along with the rest of the British, had repeatedly heard about life under the duress of occupation on the radio, in the papers and on the cinema screens, as well as having it drummed into them by the Military Intelligence people about what they might experience when they penetrated behind the enemy lines or if they were captured. It had all rather been taken for granted—part of the profession they had adopted, slightly unreal until you actually studied the taut-faced man who had been hunted and to whom freedom was still not assured. As he encountered the incomprehensible, the first hint dawned of the sinister side to his work.

The two MTBs moved faster down the narrow sound, navigating by recognised landmarks and the fixed shore lights—crews alert but easier of mind now they were on the move. Happier, too, on MTB 619 as Herlofson gave the order to start dropping the mines down the chutes, to rid themselves of these unpopular globes, with their 25 lb of explosives. Like toad's spawn, strung together by rope in bunches of five, they offended Norwegian eyes—as a menace to the MTB when aboard, a mortal danger to frail Norwegian fishing boats while adrift, and unsatisfactory even if an enemy ship did strike one because the incident would go unseen. The fluvial mine's one saving grace was its self-destructive time fuse which detonated after five days and eliminated a menace to friendly folk.

The cove on the island of Gjeiterøy in which they camouflaged themselves was one long known to the Norwegians as an excellent hiding place for MTBs and instantly recognised by Godwin as the very place to hide a coble. An ideal and almost deserted area with plenty of cover for men and tents among rocks and heather, with splended observation posts of surrounding waters. Visits by the Germans were infrequent, said the handful of inhabitants who, nevertheless, lived in dread of the invaders and of the half dozen or so local Quislings. Fynn had noticed in November that it took tact and persuasion to overcome the reluctance of a cautious people to provide such vital information that the watch post at Tungodden, which overlooked the Sogne Sea, had, so they thought, been evacuated by the Germans after a recent bombardment by MTBs.

As peaceful a scene as it was from the excellent hillside observation post overlooking the cove and the surrounding sea, the task of the watchers was by no means rewarding or pleasant. The odd fishing boat, a few small coasters and one 4,000-ton ship with two single-engine fighters flying around in the encroaching mist was all of interest they saw. For the rest of the time it was a matter of combatting the cold and wet by regular reliefs and plentiful meals.

The unwaterproofed, windproof suits helped keep out the cold, but let in the wet. Rubber-soled boots, good for rock climbing, also soon let in the damp while snow dazzle from prolonged use of binoculars shortened the time a man could spend on watch. By nightfall they all felt they had had enough without commensurate return in the sighting of targets worth attacking. Disappointed as Herlofson and Waggett were, they patiently assumed their opportunity would come. But that might depend, as always, upon good weather, and that evening, as they sat down to plan for the next day, the forecast was plain bad. Looking back on it, indeed, they would say that the arrival of that message marked the point at which their misfortunes really began.

While in enemy waters, of course, MTBs were forbidden to use their radio transmitters except to report something of vital importance, such as the sighting of a major enemy warship at sea. It was taken for granted that the signal would be detected and the transmitter's position accurately located by enemy direction-finding equipment, with swift and dire consequences. So the main function of the radio operators was to monitor broadcasts from Scapa Floe (without acknowledgement) and, above all, pick up the regular weather forecasts which were justifiably renowned for accuracy. The one for 24 February told of south-westerly winds at force 6 or more (the sort which piled up water in the mouth of the fjord), and of the likelihood of snow to reduce visibility and perhaps make conditions humanly unbearable. But not bad enough, Waggett and Godwin concluded at 0500 hours next day, to call off the aggressions of the day. Exactly to forecast, it was blowing hard when Waggett, with Corporal Solum, two of his commandos and four sailors, launched the skiff and began to row 4 miles towards Stokkevaag, and Godwin with Sergeant Bjornsted and Ordinary Seaman West started in the canoe to reconnoitre the watchpost at Tungodden, three miles off.

Godwin got back two hours later shaken and angry. In the barely ruffled water under the island's lee, progress had been good. Caught by the heavy swell and the wind funnelling into the Sogne Sea, it was another matter, taxing the thrust and balancing talents of all three paddlers to the limit. And the limit for Sergeant Bjornsted was low, based as it was upon short experience and a total ignorance of how to react in extreme conditions. Instead of putting more weight into his work he began to flag, slowing his strokes when the frail craft lurched, instead of pushing hard to maintain momentum and stability—at about 0530 hours, as Tungodden came in sight, stopping as if petrified, thus throwing the others into a tangle of paddles. Godwin thought they were finished, but there was no time to be frightened. Shouting in desperation and beating the Norwegian on the back, while West did all he could to struggle free, they awaited the fatal yaw leading to capsizing without the slightest chance of recovery by a crew, one of whom was neutralised and apparently inept. Their lives quite literally hung in the balance, before Bjornsted loosened up and paddled again, only to repeat the process a few minutes later shortly before they moved into calmer waters. West had nothing to say out loud. That was Godwin's prerogative—quickly and sharply delivered, for already the watch post was in sight about 100 yards distant. Broken water and the wind's noise naturally provided protection against being seen or heard, but their training and sense of professional pride demanded that in the presence of the enemy the full regimen should be practised in order to complete the job quickly and unobserved.

The watch post, Godwin noted, had about it an air of desolation. All windows out. Holes in the walls. Wireless mast shot away. No gun or any sign of life. The MTB gunners had done a good job. Obviously it was abandoned. There was no need to go ashore, so they turned for home, this time with Bjornsted as a passenger to enable West and himself uninterrupted use of their paddles. So far so good, thought Herlofson, even if the young officer seemed rather disgusted and, if remarks from Bjornsted were to be believed, somewhat impulsive to risk paddling in such rough water. The Tungodden drama would go the rounds below deck in MTB 619 and eventually pass into legend among the flotilla and the commandos. Sceptically, the Norwegians, with a cautious reticence as well as a certain admiration, would nickname him Hjortenfotm, meaning Running Deer or Lightfoot. As for Andrew West (the only other person to see Godwin in action in a crunch), he kept his opinion to himself, for the time being, although there was no doubt in his mind that his officer had done the right thing in trying to do his job and then saving their lives. Later the young Scotsman would argue the case in Godwin's favour:

> 'He wasn't doing nothing daft. It was dead easy if we just kept going, a pushover if everybody paddled hard. Any of our lot would have done it. Bjornsted's not bad, but its bloody daft sending us blokes who don't know what they're doing. Sub-Lieutenant Godwin's OK. He'll not do anything daft or drop us in the shit if he can help it.'

An hour later, when the skiff came alongside, Herlofson had reason to revise his opinion of boating in these conditions, when four bedraggled sailors announced, with mock pride, they had been swimming. Apparently before putting the commandos ashore at Stokkevaag, the skiff had struck a rock, tipping them all into the water. Quickly they had righted it, and reached Stokkevaag where they called on a family known to one of MTB 619's crew. The family were kindness itself, giving warm socks to everyone before the skiff started back, and offering to guide Waggett and his party to a suitable place for observing the watch post on top of the 1000-foot hill called Kletten, which they intended to attack that night.

That night Herlofson embarked the commandos from MTB 627 and made for Stokkevaag, while MTB 627 got ready to lay mines at about the same time as the attack on Kletten went in. But when Waggett came aboard with his party at Stokkevaag it was to state the need for a change of plan. The route from Stokkevaag to Kletten was terrible, he said. It took one and a half hours in daylight to cover a mere two miles. It was necessary, therefore, to land elsewhere, so they had to go back to Gjeiterøy to tell 627 about the delay before proceeding to the new landing place. On the way Waggett explained his plan, which was simplicity itself. While Godwin cut the telephone line from the enemy's billet in a hamlet called Stensund and attacked the billet, Waggett would lead an assault on Kletten, kill the Germans on duty and wreck the place. The commandos were on deck as Herlofson groped in pitch blackness under lowering clouds and a stiffening wind to locate the narrow channel between two small islands. The wind was steadily increasing in strength and the commandos raring to go when Herlofson came face to face with the perils of the situation. Not only was the wind force 7, so as to make the transfer to shore in two skiff loads extremely difficult, it was, according to the latest weather forecast, getting worse. Calling Waggett to the bridge, he explained that if the landing went ahead the chances of re-embarkation after the enemy were all stirred up might be impossible. The land force would be thrown into jeopardy. Indeed, with so strong a wind rising, it might well be impossible for the MTBs to leave the fjord. He was sorry to disappoint them but:

> 'Do you know that some of our boats have suffered cracked ribs in heavy seas? I simply cannot take that risk. It would be madness to draw attention to ourselves to compel us putting to sea to escape. I do hope you understand.'

Waggett most certainly did. He already had the greatest admiration for the manner in which Herlofson and Henrickson had navigated and handled their boats in extremely difficult conditions. But Godwin, although keeping his peace at first, was clearly disappointed.

> 'A pity' [he grumbled to Waggett in private], 'it was a good plan.'
> 'Yes' [had replied Waggett, already aware of his companion's mounting disenchantment with Norwegians in general, and anxious to quell trouble]. 'But look here, Jo, we've a couple of days before packing up. Plenty of time for another go. It would be plain silly to write off two MTBs and their crews—and us—just for the satisfaction of blowing up some concrete and killing a few Huns. We've not done badly, you know. You've done your stuff at Tungodden. I've found tons of gen about what the Germans are up to and how many there are. I've even got the names and addresses of a whole bunch of Quislings, seven of 'em. So take it easy. Our turn will come, never fear.'

Waggett need not have worried too much about Godwin's ill-concealed impatience. The sub-lieutenant's straightforward manner matched the inherent forthrightness of the Norwegians themselves. And who were they to complain about an ally whom, apparently, nothing would deter? Very well, thought Herlofson, he may be impulsive and eschew caution, but surely that strong intense personality with the grim simplicity of a desire to fight the Germans and do as much damage as possible was what they were in business for.

Unfortunately, for the next two days the weather made it impossible to let him loose. As it worsened, they were pinned to the vessel, able only to step ashore to take turns in the observation post, yet hosts to an endless succession of fishermen as news of the MTB's presence spread among the local community. They came by the row boat load, sometimes alone, occasionally in parties, and they brought with them an acute thirst for truth along with copies of the German controlled newspapers as examples of the subterfuge and downright lies of their oppressors who were, at that very moment, in the midst of yet another attempt to raise Quisling to supreme power. They yearned for news of friends who had escaped to Britain and relished this fleeting contact with fellow countrymen who were at liberty to fight the Germans with powerful weapons. And as for the German garrisons in these outlying parts—well it did rather seem as if the fishermen underestimated them, perhaps because they were so few in number and so rarely visited the tiny hamlets on the smallest islands and peninsulas. Herlofson was content to welcome these dour but friendly men, to gather information and to repay it with hope for the future at the turning point of the war. At the same time he remained alert against any who might shiftily attempt to avoid coming aboard, intercepting them and making sure they were so thoroughly compromised by a contact that it would make them think several times before reporting to the enemy. Socialising like this was a serious business, but it did have its lighter and even more poignant moments. As, for instance, when a softer, excited change in the tone of conversation on deck announced that two girls had arrived; a presence with a purpose as noted to Herlofson by a tap on his door and the sight of a petty officer, flushed and with a formal request for permission for shore leave.

'Only to the village, sir' [said the man, fumbling with his cap]. 'Not far. We can row. There will be dancing, you know. They would like us there. Not for long, of course. We would soon be back, sir. The men would like it.'

It was difficult to refuse. The pangs of long separation from home and the yearning for women who spoke the same language were plain to be seen. They both knew the risks, and knew, too, the proper answer. But the petty officer was bound to make the request, since the crew consensus demanded it. And Herlofson was bound to give it consideration before refusing. That was the way their democracy worked and was what they were fighting for. Furthermore, the men would claim, it would be sad to disappoint the brave girls who had rowed so far in ghastly weather to make them welcome. It was Norway at its best and touched him deeply. But the answer still had to be no—with regret of course.

There was much for Godwin and Waggett to learn from this period of enforced inactivity in all its pent-up boredom. For one thing, what a menace the local populace could be to lying-up parties, and therefore why it was essential to select hides only on isolated uninhabited islands. For another, how useful, vital indeed, Norwegian linguists were in communicating not only with friends, but also in a jam with the enemy. There was the occasion when Corporal Solum, out in the skiff with Waggett and a British crew, and surprised by the unexpected appearance of a patrol boat bearing down on them, had saved the day.

> 'Go on rowing. Behave like fishermen' he had said. 'Ignore them. Let me do the talking.'

It had been a tense moment, but Solum got the right approach. An exchange of greetings in Norwegian, commiserations about the weather and complaints of its effect on the catch. A friendly tone had been enough to placate the patrol boat captain, who had not even bothered to close in and examine them in detail. Which was perhaps fortunate for him, since the other members of the skiff, bent over the oars, had weapons cocked and were as trigger-happy as could be.

The weather, not the Germans, or their orders, controlled them. The third day it blew force 9 while they revised the attack on Kletten and considered also taking out a watch-post on Hugøy. The fourth they spent watching passing convoys and sending men ashore to find 20 gallons of water to replace their dwindling stocks. But an attempt that night to reconnoitre Tungodden, to discover what three Norwegian workmen had been doing there during the day, was called off due to high wind and pitch blackness. It was only slightly better next morning, but good enough for Waggett, Godwin and Solum, in thick mist, with grim determination, to land from a canoe on Ravnø and, in the persistent heavy swell, reach the Tungodden peninsular. There, once more, the same conditions which had almost overcome Godwin prevented a landing. Moreover, the bigger skiff with a party of six could do no better that night, Waggett concluding that 'a landing would have proved extremely difficult and the return journey impossible. With great difficulty we returned to the MTBs.'

At this stage a note of desperation and a sensation of being trapped is to be found in the reports of all concerned. 'The obvious conclusions we may draw from these uncompleted reconnaissances', admitted Godwin, 'is that when the weather forecasts sent to us from the Shetlands are bad for the MTBs it is equally bad for us to operate from small craft.' But next day, as the wind continued to gust and with visibility poor, a new worry intruded. 'Another water party brought fresh supplies aboard. Fishermen again visited us and brought more newspapers, also sold us fish. Food stocks very low.'

To his chagrin, Herlofson had to tell Waggett that starvation loomed ahead.

'It is the rationing regulations' [he explained in disgust]. 'They sent us on this three day operation with only three days food in reserve. I know it sounds stupid, but, of course, nobody foresaw how it might be impossible to get away.'

The mere suggestion that they were running short was enough to make them feel hungry, let alone suffer from the actual detrimental effects of reduced nutrition. As the galley cherished every crumb and as every mouthful was eaten as if the last, the pathology of hunger began to overcome their bodies and, as a symptom, their resistance to cold: experiencing, in fact, the initial stage of a classic decline in 'resting metabolic rate' when the intake of energy was so restricted as to lead by degrees to the point at which the body, unable to satisfy its need for energy, began to feed upon its own tissue and thus induce an accelerated wasting away towards a skeletal condition.

Each man pleaded with the weather, gauging the wind and watching the skies while willing a change. Time dragged from forecast to forecast, which alternately raised and lowered their hopes. The forecast for day 7, 1 March, was sickenenly adverse, but next morning there were unmistakable signs of improvement, to the extent that Herlofson and Waggett decided to attack Kletten that night before returning home. Three hours later a reversion to flux when the next report suggested the improvement would not last. Shortly their unease increased when a visiting fisherman reported that the Germans had heard the MTBs during their first attempt on Kletten and had at once manned the post. Of course, the enemy might now think the MTBs had gone. On the other hand, it was noticeable that shipping movements round and about had suddenly ceased. Maybe it was because the fluvial mines, at the end of their five-day period of activity, were beginning automatically to detonate, but perhaps it portended something more sinister, such as an attack upon their hide.

Waggett weighed up the weather and recommended that the attack should go ahead. Herlofson hedged his bets. He slipped from the hide in daylight to make a dash for the sea, before the weather again deteriorated, and kept open the options of attacking Kletten providing he could enter the Indre Stensund on the way to the landing place, but always ready to make at once for the Shetlands before the food ran out completely.

As they left the shelter of the land at 1800 hours, the wind force rose to 7 and it began to snow. Immediately it was apparent that to navigate the tricky entrance to the Indre Stensund was far too risky. Turning northwards and then into the open sea on a westerly course, the full fury of the gale struck them—winds between force 8 and 9, the waves pounding the boats, whipping up drenching, icy spray and threatening to engulf them, the snow lashing the faces of the men straining their eyes on the bridge, while the majority below prayed and vomitted. Thirty minutes of that was enough for Herlofson and Henrickson. Together they turned about, lurching violently, beam on, and ran for the nearest shelter which promised a reasonable hiding place—the island of Aspøy.

The chart indicated the Dybesund, a narrow channel which those with local knowledge said would lead to a good hide. Darkness was falling and so entrance had to be made at once. Hands were posted forward to give warning of obstructions as they moved slowly in, guns were manned to cope with an unexpected welcome, commandos stood ready for a quick landing as they touched. A cry from the bows, 'Mine under the starboard bow', lost nothing in its frightening urgency upon the British despite the fact that it was shouted in Norwegian. Herlofson's quick move to the starboard side of the bridge was countered by an involuntary shifting to port of the majority. Waggett saw it, a whopper with long black horns bobbing about on the surface and about to disappear under the bows. It had to touch. In the imagination of some it did! Yet a few seconds later, lasting a year, it reappeared, floating insolently astern and, all being well, out to sea.

There is a sense of ancient history straight from the days of sail in Herlofson's log entry for 2000 hours:

> 'Made fast. Camouflaged both ships. Ate last of ships biscuits.'

Waggett's entry for 21.30 is more expressive of the straits to which they had come:

> 'Had a conference about food. We now have no bread, sugar, milk, butter, potatoes; there is just enough left for two meals after which, if we are still here, sheep will be killed.'

What Waggett really meant was that the British, not their allies, would kill a sheep, practising for the first time in deadly earnest the survival techniques they had been taught with commando knives at Achnacarry. For the Norwegians were totally averse to the attempt. They had debated it with asperity in the sort of 'parliament' they liked to hold with officers and petty officers whenever something tricky of a non-operational nature cropped up. This sort of thing to Waggett was irksome and a negation of normal military practice— the British way. To Godwin it was a lot worse, an infuriating prevarication which wasted time and undermined an officer's authority. On this occasion there stood revealed what Godwin would call typical Norwegian half-heartedness to war. It made no sense to him, with hunger twisting his bowels and the cold shaking his body, that they rejected hunting for food. They said they were objecting to stealing from their fellow countrymen. He replied that putting peacetime morality before war's stark necessities in an emergency was ridiculous. It was possible to respect the probity but to disagree vehemently with the vote which decided Herlofson to forbid sheep stealing, a decision which Waggett, with legal correctitude as a British Military Force Commander, ignored.

Next morning they still were there. The wind had risen to force 8 or 9, whipping up the sea to greater violence than ever. At 0830 hours, two parties set out, one to find water, the other, under Waggett, for sheep. As he went over the side a petty officer looked him in the eye and said 'If you catch one, we will not eat it.' And Waggett had looked back, with equal sincerity and replied: 'If, when you smell it cooking, you change your mind, we will not hold it against you.'

Water they found in plenty, 40 gallons of it, but no sheep. Either there were none being grazed on this unpopulated island or the sheep had done the sensible thing and taken cover against the terrible weather. But this day, when Herlofson authorised breaking into the emergency Bully Beef packs contained in the emergency floats, the temporary avoidance of a breach of Anglo-Norwegian relations was the only compensation. Their hunger was excruciating. Every morsel was a repast, chewed with relish no matter how unappetising it looked. The stress of under-nutrition induced attitudes which previously belonged only to the pages of explorers' tales of extremities in the Arctic wastes. Famine, such as their condition seemed to equate, had previously figured only as reports they had read in newspapers about some outlandish corner of the globe. It was inconceivable that they should be compelled to endure such deprivation in civilised Europe, within sight of hospitable homes which the circumstances placed out of bounds—and a unique situation they were determined, if possible, to avoid in the future.

As their suffering was prolonged and the time hung more heavily, abnormalities created uncharacteristic attitudes. Hearing the sound of a powerful diesel-powered vessel approaching from a fjord, they were fascinated to see a submarine, a British submarine, heading for the sea to submerge once she butted into the gale. Ordinarily they would have been intrigued by such a strange encounter, asking themselves what secret mission brought her there and wishing her well. But with their minds obsessed by the desire for food and warmth, there were some who enviously pictured the submariners, cosy and well fed in well-appointed surroundings, and deplored the injustice of her inconsiderately passing them by.

On the eve of the ninth night in stormbound enemy waters, a slightly more favourable weather forecast was received, encouraging them to sail at 0400 hours next day, 3 March, in sufficient time to be beyond the range of fighters by daylight. So optimistic was Herlofson, and so disgusted, too, that in nine days they had failed to strike a blow—not even fired a shot in anger—that he seriously contemplated bombarding some hapless German outpost if only to work off his feelings. But the consensus of the officers was against him. Perhaps it was the ravages of malnutrition which sapped their aggression as well as their energy; maybe it was commonsense or an intuitive reluctance to push their luck too far. After all, they had survived among the enemy with two big craft for nine days without coming to harm. That was miraculous and there was a law of averages!

Then there was the intransigent sea which locked them in. The weather, at 0400 hrs, although showing signs of improvement, remained unfavourable. So they waited two hours, thus beyond the time when it would be unsafe against day fighters, until at 0605 hrs Herlofson abandoned prudence. He 'slipped and proceeded', regardless of the state of the sea or the fear of a prowling Messerschmitt, resolved to escape before, as some believed (pessimistically and unscientifically), they might be destroyed by hunger. It was touch and go, an hour's grim balancing of engines and rudder against the wiles of nature before they won free, a time in which Herlofson and Henrickson demonstrated accomplished boat-handling techniques to an exceptional degree as MTBs lunged, twisted and turned their way through a barrier of watery upheaval before at last reaching slightly calmer waters. A period of turmoil in which, fearing engulfment, Henrickson jettisoned the mines he had never found the opportunity to lay. It was a befitting irony at the end of a sterile visit home.

Godwin is matter of fact in his report, simply recording that it was 'rough'. Waggett, however, took the opportunity to offer his thanks for their deliverance.

> 'At this point I do not think it out of place to mention the great skill with which the Commanding Officers of the MTBs navigated their craft throughout our stay in narrow and dangerous waters.'

And at 1830 hrs, with relief:

> 'Arrived at Lerwick, Shetland, and disembarked.'

PLATE 6.   A Klepper canoe of improved design to those used by 14 Commando
with special locating equipment

PLATE 7. Norwegian Fairmile D MTBs set out on patrol

PLATE 8. LCP coble

PLATE 9. Klepper canoes

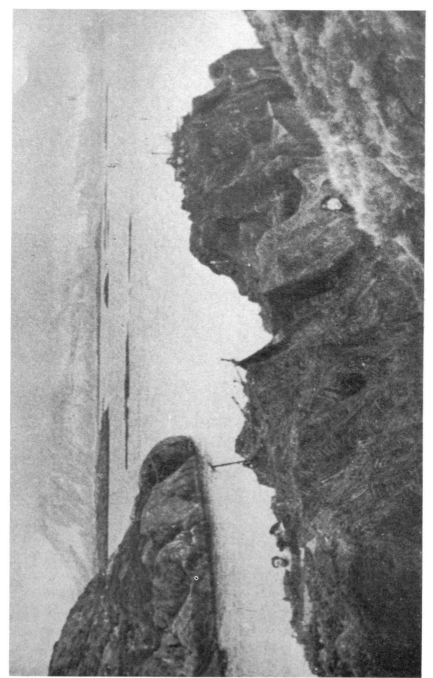

PLATE 10.   Camouflaged MTBs in a fjord

8

The Thraldom of CRACKERS

When it came to writing their reports, after taking a bath and eating their first solid meal in nearly a week, the four officers concerned—Herlofson and Henrickson, Waggett and Godwin—had two aims. To render an accurate account of what had taken place and to make recommendations which would help them and their successors in subsequent operations, and in greater security. It is doubtful if, for one moment, they wrote for posterity, or imagined that, one day, historians would examine their statements in the Public Record Office. So, unlike some among august superior officers, they were not tempted to place themselves in a better light to history. They omitted only those occurrences which might reflect gratuitously against individuals or, possibly, undermine security. Therefore, there is no mention of the failure to attempt a last moment attack on the enemy or the sighting of that mysterious submarine.

Godwin's strictures about his Norwegian canoe mate were emphasised, however, in a sweeping generalisation at the end of his report, an onslaught which tells us rather more about him than the Norwegians:

> 'As regards boats the Norwegians are useless: they do not appear to have any guts for this kind of work. This may sound like plain talking but after nearly being drowned by the Sergeant at half past five in the morning this is how I feel' (*sic*).

Unjust as this was, his invective had to be read in conjunction with the next sentence and with recommendations by Herlofson and Waggett in their reports:

> 'But I would like to say that given the smallest degree of luck in the weather, canoes and other small craft of a similar nature, are well worth while, in fact we considered them essential for moving about in these waters' (*sic*).

For their part, Herlofson and Henrickson, in the joint report dictated to Lieutenant Job for Vice Admiral Wells and the Admiralty, thought: 'MTBs can remain on the Norwegian coast for long periods providing there is sufficient food, and that there is the minimum of communication with people ashore'—an opinion amplified by Waggett when he wrote:

> 'This operation has proved that we can lay up in a good hideout for long periods . . . here are excellent targets for a party with "limpets". . . . These suggestions were discussed fully with the Commanding Officer of MTB 619 and he is in support of these suggestions. In his opinion it is *not* necessary to return to base immediately after a Watchpost or similar target has been assaulted; it is necessary though to proceed to a new hideout and this is possible.'

He went on to say how keen he and Herlofson were to do more operations of this nature.

At the completion of CRACKERS and the start of discussions with Waggett, Major Fynn, Major Collins and Lieutenant Job, something more than a page turned in Godwin's saga. It marked the end of a chapter, really a prologue to the immortal events to come as his thoughts, interlocking with those of his associates, set in train revised ideas, linked to the coble and built into the concept which was to become Operation CHECKMATE. The challenge of carrying out a lying-up operation with coble and Klepper canoe now took him in thrall. He wanted to get started at once and before the ink was dry on his report was pestering Fynn and Job to get things moving. But Fynn who was keen, was also simultaneously preparing the next attack on Norway, Operation ROUNDABOUT, along with the preliminary arrangements for more to follow. 30th Flotilla was approaching a climax in its activities (keeping Job at full stretch) as Vice Admiral Wells sought to achieve all the success he could before the equinox and shorter nights made the MTBs' task too difficult. So Godwin found himself in a backwater, almost at a loose end. Unable to win immediate wholehearted acceptance of his scheme, he could only cogitate and refine a technique as yet unproven.

Apart from lobbying his superiors whenever the opportunity occurred, Godwin retrained his 'gang' and lavished care upon the coble as if, said Waggett, it were his wife. He mixed business with pleasure too, on occasion. There was the time he and Waggett, needing to dispose of some old made-up explosives, decided to go fishing in one of the canoes to boost their rations. Godwin sat on the bank priming the charges while Waggett dropped the first over the side and awaited results. Unfortunately he had forgotten about shock waves which not only killed the fish but partly blew the bottom out of the canoe. Waggett recalled that 'Godwin nearly collapsed with mirth as I paddled madly for the shore and stepped out with water running out of my backside—

the canoe I regret was a write-off and earned me a severe ticking off for not wearing my Mae West.'

On another occasion Godwin and Waggett took part in an impromptu concert party singing a duet of *Lydia Pink* in which he, Godwin, 'was tremendous'. Lighthearted interludes provided respite to the all-consuming involvement with explosives and boats, offset by planning in a vacuum and the dreary waiting for a positive response to his proposals. Moreover, impatience was sharpened by the news of fresh victories in Russia and in North Africa, and, within a short while, the news that his brother had been severely wounded at the Battle of Mareth with the loss of a leg. In retrospect he would remember those March days at Lerwick as a welcome interlude as the opportunity for lighthearted diversions ran out.

Between the sending out and welcoming home of VP and OMNIBUS operations, Fynn, Job and Collins studied a variety of projects, such as the blowing up of power stations and ships, the releasing of Russian prisoners of war—all to be carried out by parties which might stay ashore for three weeks. At the same time, SOE, copying its earlier successful operation by March-Phillips and Appleyard to steal two ships from the neutral harbour of Fernando Po, was trying, with Norwegian agents, to cut out merchant ships from harbours, right under the enemy's nose. On 15 March Herlofson returned from Aarebraat in MTB 619, triumphantly announcing that he had sunk a large vessel with torpedoes to make up with a bang for the frustrations of CRACKERS. On another VP, Mayor and Burgess were included for experience and found out how rough the sea could be off Norway.

But greatly improved German defences were making operations extremely hazardous. Watchposts were being extended, batteries strengthened and a warning system linked by radar and air patrols developed. Fishing beyond a 50-mile limit had been forbidden and the control of off-shore movement tightened up by the sudden imposition of check points and searches, the unannounced creation of arbitrary 'forbidden zones' at sea and curfews on land. Already these measures were hurting the fishing craft of the Shetland Bus, compelling abandonment of their operations in April and transfer of their functions to the MTBs. At the same time, the shorter nights were hampering the MTBs, preventing them from tarrying in enemy waters, making the lurk an unacceptable risk. ACOS thought it might just, but only just, be practical to employ a small 60-foot MTB when it became available in May. But if the attacks on enemy shipping passing through the Inner Leads were to be continued by means other than minelaying throughout the summer months, a less conspicuous kind of lying up vessel was required. With that in mind, Collins arranged on 15 March to send 15 Klepper canoes to Lerwick.

As the enemy and the hours of daylight obtruded, the Norwegian relationship applied brakes on aggression of another kind. As information accumulated of the latest bid by Quisling to win approval for his bogus suzerainty and false claim that Norway was no longer in a formal state of war with Germany, the anxiety of King Haakon and his government, and their wish to mitigate the pressures upon their people at home until this latest political initiative had failed, was expressed. They feared that widespread guerrilla attacks would provoke massed terrorism and reprisals which might reverse the rising tide of patriotism and turn back the waverers already 'rowing' in the king's direction. Understandably, the British government sympathised with these fears and was anxious, while prosecuting the war with all vigour, to avoid irresponsible trivial raids for raiding's sake during this crisis. So when Major Collins applied his mind to recommendations for future operations, he had to bear in mind the Norwegian people. In a letter on 9 March to Fynn and Waggett, congratulating the latter on the CRACKERS report and the work done by the commando party, he included a warning which was to influence both Godwin and CHECKMATE.

> 'It is this question of contact with local Norwegians. I know in some cases it may be essential, on this operation it certainly was, in order to get supplies and the information obtained from them was really useful. Yet the risk of security is a very dangerous one, not perhaps so much for the immediate operation but fear of the Germans finding out details of your force, and setting a trap for future occasions.'

By a process of elimination, Operation CHECKMATE took shape. To begin with, in Godwin's mind, by the elimination of Norwegian participation within his party—not so much because of the higher political ramifications (which probably he was hardly made aware of), but chiefly because of the threat they imposed to themselves and anybody visibly connected to them. He did so not simply because he dismissed them as 'useless', or 'without guts for this kind of work', or even because of their implied threat to raider's security, as postulated by Collins on behalf of COHQ. He had also to bear in mind the current German interpretation of the legal status of Norwegians engaged in hostilities, as presented by MI 9, the War Office Branch which dealt with prisoners of war. They imagined the Germans arguing on the lines that:

> 'The leader of Norway is Quisling. He is recognised by the Germans, but has no army at his disposal. Therefore any Norwegian in uniform is to be treated as a *franc-tireur*.'

Furthermore, it was believed by MI 9 that even commandos would not be regarded as soldiers, and this prompted detailed contemplation of the Hitler Commando Order and British measures to circumvent it. The full text of the Order exposing commandos and their ilk to the death penalty contained caveats stating:

> 'This order does not apply to the treatment of any soldiers who, in the

course of normal hostilities . . . are captured in battle or give themselves up. Nor does this order apply to enemy soldiers falling into our hands after battles at sea. . . .'

Already, of course, it was known that the Commando Order has been invoked to shoot, out of hand, commandos and Norwegians who had been captured recently. To Godwin, as to most of those engaged in raiding, the threat of the Commando Order was simply an additional risk in a very dangerous game which they had volunteered to play fully in the realisation they might be killed. It posed no greater a deterrent than other enemy defensive measures. But awareness of immunities to the Commando Order and of the Geneva Conventions were valid. It was desirable to dress and act as soldiers or sailors in battle and totally to exclude any connection with Norwegians if that averted any accusation that they were *franc-tireurs*, commandos or Norwegians—proof of which misdemeanours would make them subject to the death penalty. For this reason, along with all the others from the outset, he was determined to resist the inclusion of Norwegians in the CHECKMATE party, regardless of their invaluable knowledge of the country and its people; sacrificing, too, their vital function as interpreters among rural people and fishermen, few of whom, unlike the townspeople, understood English.

The selection of the target area was governed, also, by elimination. It would be wrong to send Godwin and his men to a place where shipping did not frequently anchor, which was too heavily defended, which was exposed to rough water, in which suitable hiding places in virtually unpopulated terrain or islands did not exist, and which was so far from Lerwick as to over-prolong passage. These considerations effectively disposed of the distant north, the more strongly defended and densely populated south and the enticing but exposed central Sognefjord region. As the sector closest to Shetland, that left the myriad of headlands and large and small islands between Bergen and Stavanger, a stretch of water occasionally visited by MTBs during VP operations and one in which enemy shipping regularly anchored at frequent intervals for working or protection. Looking closer at the charts, the choice of Godwin, Job and the rest at last fell emphatically on a piece of enclosed water called the Karmøysund, separating the islands of Karmøy and Fosenøy (which shipping using the Leads could not safely by-pass), with the small ports of Haugesund at the northern end and of Kopervik at the southern one. Here, it was thought, shipping frequently did anchor for the night. The defences, although quite strong, were apparently by no means impenetrable. Here, too, in an area more densely populated than, for example, the mouth of the Sognefjord, there were many unpopulated coves in which coble and canoes could be hidden within striking distance of the anchorages.

There were, of course, several other operations also under consideration. When Collins visited Lerwick at the beginning of April he was to discuss with

Wells, Job and Fynn such prospects as GUNHOUSE (in which commandos would be inserted by Catalina flying boat) and FLYFORD (the setting up of a guerrilla base on Stord). But it was Godwin's scheme to which he devoted most space, relative to the rest, when he wrote his report on 7 April, and which found most favour in London to be graced, at last, with its own code name— CHECKMATE. 'ACOS and Lt Job', wrote Collins, 'are keen and they requested intelligence to be obtained.' Their rough plan proposed an operation towards the end of the present moon period, end of April. One MTB would disembark the military force in a small skiff a few miles north of Haugesund and hide in a sheltered creek. Klepper canoes would then attack shipping with limpets, return to the skiff and eventually be picked up by MTBs. 'Suggested Force Commander—Lt Godwin RNVR, 14 Cdo who will probably be in London next week.'

From this document among several, it is evident that Vice Admiral Wells, as well as Job, was impressed by Godwin, perhaps because he had met him more than once. Indeed, there were few among those involved in the planning who were not, although Leif Utne stated his objections on the grounds that the coble (Collins's skiff) would be a giveaway. 'We would also attach personal reservations. There was too much fantasy in the plan, not enough reality—a typically British attempt to perform something brilliantly unproven.' Further-more, Godwin was lacking in self-criticism—as may well have been the impression given by Godwin to any Norwegian who exhibited the slightest reservations, thus automatically becoming subject to his castigation of Nor-wegians as 'useless' with no 'guts' for this kind of work.

Godwin's visit to London practically coincided with the delivery of a Most Secret letter from Vice Admiral Wells to the Admiralty, with copies to the C-in-C Home Fleet, Chief of Combined Operations (Mountbatten) and Naval Intelligence. And as so frequently was the case upon meeting strong characters for the first time, Godwin made hardly any impression upon M. R. D. Foot, who provided an intelligence briefing, or Colonel Robert Neville, who was Mountbatten's Chief Coordinating Planner at COHQ. But as also was typical, his reaction to being overawed by a sceptical reception stiffened his resolve and drove him silently along the self-assumed path of destiny. In all probability, too, he knew that Vice Admiral Wells's forceful support would guarantee CHECKMATE's adoption—that senior officer having reached an accord with Godwin while taking time to get to know him and form a high opinion.

Departmental politics tipped the scales. Despite their expressed reser-vations, neither Mountbatten nor Neville were prepared to rebuff an Admiral who was positively eager to raid at a time when a majority of his kind tended to obstruct COHQ. Moreover, Wells argued forcefully with a shrewd conclusion taken from the SOE report on CARHAMPTON, pointing out that if the Norwegian operatives had been armed with limpets they could have sunk several ships, including two submarines, instead of failing to achieve anything by an abortive attempt at 'cutting out'. He went on:

> 'With this in view, and with the object of intensification of the attack
> on the enemy life line to North Norway, I propose the following:
> (a) That a Force of these men, trained to the use of "Limpets" with
>   suitable boats, be stationed in Shetland to operate with the MTBs.
> (b) Operation orders to be drawn up jointly with SOE's representative
>   in Shetland.'

By the time Godwin had arrived back in Lerwick, CHECKMATE was not
only agreed in principle but was within days of formal approval. The hesitancy
of the past month was swept away and, as was all too frequent on these
occasions, the final arrangements had to be made in haste since the earliest
starting date was fixed for 23 April, less than a fortnight hence, with 2 May as
the last day practical within that phase of the moon.

9

Setting Him to Get On with It

The rules of the raiding game laid it down that only people with a need to know were told the details of any operation. Above all, time, place and objectives were subject to the very tightest scrutiny. For that reason, Godwin, who was extremely security conscious and never told his brother about his work, was forbidden to discuss with even his closest colleague, Ken Waggett, the details of CHECKMATE. But that did not prevent discussion of general practices concerning the sort of coble and canoe project which had long interested them. They compared notes on the equipment needed, the stores to be packed into the coble, modifications to the craft, weapons to be carried, special training to be carried out and the men required. It was with regard to training and men that Waggett made his most valuable contribution.

> 'Look, Jo' [Waggett had said before CHECKMATE had become an official code name on COHQ's books]. 'Look, you've carried out that loading and towing trial, I know. But that's just a beginning. What you want next is a full scale try out, a rehearsal if you like. Stow the coble with everything you'll take on the day. Do as realistic a trial run as can be arranged. You know; if possible have the same MTB as will tow you across. Pick you up outside the harbour. Go for a swan round at the speeds likely to see how the coble rides. Drop off into a hide at night. Do a dummy attack in the canoes on the ships here at Lerwick, with the guards warned to keep a sharp look-out and report anything they see. After that, back to the hide followed by MTB pick up and home. Simulate everything you can. That way you may lay most of the gremlins and see what's missing and what's superfluous.'

Probably Godwin would have done something like that in any case. He agreed at once. But maybe the next idea would not have occurred to him:

> 'OK! Next let me put it frankly and say that there's something not

quite right with you and your lot. You're a grand bunch; watermanship's fine. Fit as fleas. You're also dab hands at explosives and limpets and all that sort of thing. But on land you're ducks out of water! What I mean is this, you've no real idea how to soldier—what to do in a fire fight, how to set an ambush and how to make best use of your weapons—and I'll come back to them again in a minute. Jo, what you need is an instructor. One to take your field craft in hand—to make soldiers of you and give you a chance if it comes to a shooting match.'

They talked around it. Godwin had to be persuaded that being a saboteur was not in itself enough. Moreover, his initial plan to leave one man alone in the coble—probably Petty Officer Hiscock—while the others took off in the canoes began to look weak.

'Have you anybody in mind?' [he asked].
'Yes. There's a sergeant in 12 Commando. One of the best. Very keen, first class shot, skier, good instructor. And a no-nonsense chap with bags of guts.'

Godwin nodded and agreed to try him. He also agreed at once to Waggett's next suggestion, that the pistols and sten guns with which they were currently armed would be useless beyond point blank range.

'You'll hit nothing over 12 feet with that toy' [expostulated Waggett]. 'And the sten's not much better. Twenty yards if you're lucky and a few stoppages thrown in. What you need is a Bren. Accurate, reliable and real killing power to any range you're likely to want—you know?'

Godwin's memory went back to the healthy kick of the Bren guns he had fired during the voyage from Buenos Aires, the tracer skimming the waves. He knew.

Orders to report to Major Fynn reached Sergeant Jack Cox shortly after returning from leave. It had been quiet back at North Cadbury in Somerset, but fun to see old friends, have a few pints and take his sister to the cinema at Yeovil to see *Mrs Minerva*. She had wept as they came out and felt silly doing so at the side of her big brother. Since joining the 4th Battalion Somerset Light Infantry in 1937, Cox had become a professional soldier in every way, but bored by inaction. As patriotic and anxious as Godwin was to get at the Germans, it was not enough that he had been rapidly promoted to Sergeant and had become a leading light in the select Bren gun carrier platoon. A natural leader, he was also a disciplinarian with a sense of humour whose first act upon putting up a stripe as lance corporal was to put his younger brother on a charge for some minor military misdemeanour. Sitting around in England with his battalion had become a penance. The Commando course at Achnacarry had stretched him. He maintained that, without his officer's encouragement, he might have broken down during a forced 100-mile march. Failure was behind him. He had learnt that the art of long-distance marching was a battle of mind over fatigue in which trains of thought conquered pain—a masochism which, he believed, could be taught to others as it had been to him. As of the moment, the order to report to Major Fynn looked promising. Major Ted Fynn was a man of action actually engaged on operations. This looked like the chance to put into practice over five years training. It therefore came as a blow when he was told to report to a young naval officer and teach his lot how to be commandos—without being included in the party himself.

Cox added variety and pain to the CHECKMATE party's existence. The labours of sweating at canoe paddles soon felt like holidays in bed compared with what the commando sergeant inflicted on them in the crash infantryman's course he had been told to run. Never for one moment were they still except when it was time to sleep—and even then he was liable to have them out and on the go again. If they were not crawling through heather, engaged in unarmed combat, shooting their weapons or doubling from one place to another, they were being taught about fire and movement, how to set an ambush and how to build defensive positions of their hide. He was hard on them in the endeavour, too late, so he thought, to rub in a far more aggressive state of mind. Remorselessly he hammered away at the inculcation of the commando principle that, when other fighting men considered the time to stop had come, they went on marching, shooting and fighting just that much longer. He appreciated that Godwin and his men were bent on causing destruction for its own sake and that their leader had an admirable obsession with the coble and canoe idea. But that, in the opinion of Cox (as it was of Waggett), was insufficient. To survive Godwin, Hiscock and the others had to learn how to kill a man without hesitation—to cross the psychological barrier which prevented principled civilised men from killing a fellow human being.

The sight of Godwin and his party toiling was by now an everyday entertainment for the Norwegians of the MTB Flotilla. Jacob Børresen, the First Lieutenant of MTB 626, noted their fitness, their exceedingly high morale and gaiety under pressure. It won the admiration of the MTB crews with whom they were very popular. Friendships sprang up and were strengthened as the British learnt how to converse with and understand Norwegians whose English was still in its rudimentary stages. Indeed it was discovered that Godwin's basic German was quite useful. Such, indeed, was the enthusiasm of at least one Norwegian sailor that he volunteered, and was granted permission, to join the CHECKMATE party. Godwin refused him, of course, for although by this time he had improved his opinions of Norwegians and enjoyed their company, nothing was going to alter his determination to exclude them from the operation. In any case, the preparations for the rehearsal were indicating, what had not been apparent during the earlier trial, that space was at a premium.

To begin with, the size of the party had increased from the original five to six by including a radio operator. The need for this addition should have been clear from the outset to receive the weather forecast. Strangely, however, this was not the reason stated. Instead, his task was described as that of reporting success and arranging the date for pick-up, a signals procedure which ran contrary to normal MTB practice for fear of being located by direction-finding. The inclusion of the operator, however, depended upon finding a suitable man with the skill and aptitude to operate in these conditions—and that proved difficult. Furthermore, the size and weight of the set and batteries supplied posed considered stowage difficulties.

Prior to the rehearsal most of the stowage problems, with the exception of the radio, had been overcome. Because the coble raised a lot of spray in even a moderate sea at 7 knots, it had to be made waterproof for towing at between 15 and 20 knots. The canvas screen Godwin fitted to keep out the spray also fulfilled the equally important function of concealing the two canoes from the air or by some passing vessel. Limpets (20 per canoe), arms and ammunition, equipment and clothing, tents, food, water and medical supplies had to be packed round the men and the canoes. It was a tight squeeze, but looked workmanlike. In Børresen's opinion, the coble, as finally painted green, looked very like 'what we call a motor "snekke" without mast or sail, used both for fishing and for pleasure and are very good seaboats. Both the snekke and the kayaks were of a type very much used in Norway so they would not draw much attention even if used during daylight.'

In accordance with an exercise set by Fynn and Job, the coble, fully stowed and crewed, less the radio operator, left Lerwick and made rendezvous with the MTB outside the harbour. The transfer of the men to the MTB went smoothly. As before, the coble rode well as she bounded along in the fast boat's wake. It was not thought necessary to go far, just enough to clear the coast and make a token approach to the drop off position five miles offshore in the dark, prior to heaving-to and transferring the party from MTB to coble. Again there were no difficulties. The coble's engine started at once and Godwin set course by compass for Bressay Island to hide up for the day, before making the attempt on Lerwick harbour the following night. This time his navigation was hardly put to the test. It was a simple matter to steer from a known point of departure (fixed by the MTB) a short distance to a coastline which was almost at once in sight. Before daybreak he had identified the lying-up area and taken the coble cautiously inshore at slow speed. Soon he found a nicely sheltered inlet which was within easy paddling distance of the harbour. There they camouflaged the coble, erected and concealed the tents and took stock.

Of course, the exercise situation was unrealistic, try as Godwin did to make it otherwise. They knew the area well and where the ships anchored. Nevertheless, they tried not to cheat, setting themselves to defeat the prying eyes of observers sent out by Fynn to discover their whereabouts—and succeeding in doing so. Throughout the day, Godwin and Hiscock took it in turn to keep watch from an observation post with vision across the anchorage, plotting the position of ships for attack that night. It was reminiscent of CRACKERS but not so cold. Yet dangerous. There was always the danger somebody might take them for Germans and actually shoot them. Meanwhile, the others stood guard over the hide and kept out of sight, not daring to start unloading the canoes until last light in case they were spotted. When darkness fell they were ready and Godwin had settled and given out his plan of attack against a destroyer anchored close by the main quay. With West as his companion and Mayor and Burgess to follow in their canoe, he set forth, leaving Hiscock to his lonely vigil with the coble in the hide.

They stayed in sight of land—which would have contented Godwin's old instructor in navigation. The course took them just far enough out to avoid observation from the shore and not so far as to endanger them from ships and craft leaving and entering the harbour. When anything was heard approaching they would stop paddling and avert their blackened faces so as not to attract attention by splash or movement. From the shadows they watched fishing boats pass and once a pair of MTBs departing on some nefarious mission across the North Sea. Ahead they picked out a few shaded lights, the sounds of ships working and of merriment ashore to guide them. With Godwin leading and Mayor straining his eyes to keep in sight, they managed to glide within less than a hundred yards of the shore and the grey silhouette of the destroyer. Signing Mayor to come alongside, he gave final instructions, according to plan.

'Alright Mayor. This is it. There she is. Hold here while I have a go. Then if anything goes wrong, let things cool down a bit and you have a shot—or at something else if that looks better. OK?'
'Aye, aye, sir. And Good Luck.'

They parted, Godwin and West now using single paddles with unflurried strokes to sneak up on the destroyer, to within sound of her auxiliary machinery and that of occasional raised voices. The ruffled water and the darkness cloaked them, making the task of watchers on deck difficult, warned as they had been that something might be attempted that night. Maybe it was because they were concentrating so hard upon approaching unnoticed that Godwin arrived in something of a rush, West, in the bow position, having to backwater hurriedly to avoid ramming the ship and making a loud bump, if not holing the frail canoe. From now on it was West's job to maintain a space of 6 feet between canoe and ship by careful movements of the paddle to balance against the running tide, holding stationary while Godwin placed the limpets; both, all the time, on the alert against an indication that a sentry's suspicions had been aroused.

Without lights, Godwin had to work by practised touch, setting the acid-activated fuses of the 2-lb charges by the twist of a butterfly nut. That was simplicity itself and needed no rehearsing. Far more dexterity was required to hook each limpet to a long bamboo rod and dangle it against the ship's side, close enough for the magnets to find a hold. One clumsy jerk could draw attention or let fall the limpet into the depths. Or total failure could also be caused by fouling on the ship's plates sufficient to defeat the magnetic attraction; unlikely with a warship, greedy for speed and dependent upon cleanliness — but all too possible with some slow old merchant vessels in service. This destroyer was clean. The first limpet clunked into place after tedious fiddling terminated by an impulsive flip of the rod. The next three, spaced the length of the ship, went on quicker. Helped by West's improving sensing of the current's pull and rock-steady holding in position of the canoe, Godwin was able to exploit his angler's skill to attach them with considerable ease.

When all four limpets were in place, each with the potential to blast a six-foot diameter hole in the plate in five hours time had they been live, Godwin gave West the whisper 'Time to go', to ease off and allow the tide to carry them clear, using his paddles only to steer. Within five minutes they were paddling gently in unison through the darkness in search of Mayor's canoe, making contact without undue difficulty and setting a course by compass for the hide. They were jubilant and filled with confidence at their achievement. Moreover, they found the hide with enough time to spare to restow the canoes before daylight. That ended the exercise. The pick-up by the MTB took place a few hours later in 'peacetime' conditions, the tow home a mere formality prior to reporting to Fynn and telling Job that if the Navy cared to examine the destroyer's hull they would find four limpet mines where none should be at all. It was a triumph. CHECKMATE was proven feasible. Their reward was a fortnight's leave over Easter, a spell at home during which the demands of security were all the more vital for their survival — let alone disciplinary consequences if reported for 'careless talk'. Their leave and travel documents were issued by the shore station HMS *Fox*. Mostly they did not talk about their work to their families or friends and if asked what they did either refused to reply or gave evasive answers. Neville Burgess, for example, told a brother that he was a cook — which had a grain of truth since he was quite useful in the kitchen. His only breaches of security were the Norwegian sailor's hat with its red pom pom, which he had 'won' — thus establishing a Norwegian connection with the Shetlands — and mention to his best friend of a trip to Norway. And Keith Mayor sometimes talked a bit more than he should to his youngest sister, telling her about limpet-laying techniques from canoes and about the Norwegians whom he liked and a few of whose phrases he had acquired on the VP operation which he hinted at without giving positive information. It was hard not to share such exciting events with somebody close and to boast and have them know you were 'doing your bit'. But it was risky and against orders, a serious breach of security of the sort which few were not guilty at some time or another.

Before they went on leave, only one doubt loomed over Godwin and Petty Officer Hiscock; the fundamental matter, as was obvious, of the coble's fitness for the task. They had noticed vibration and unusual sounds coming from the engine, gearbox or the propeller shaft shortly after the tow had been cast off. Examination by an Engine Room Artificer in the harbour yard had found nothing wrong with the engine or gearbox, but evidence of overheating in one of the two bearings of the propeller shaft.

'Lack of grease—or what?' Godwin had asked in acute anxiety. If she failed they forfeited their mobile base and might even be marooned, if not cast adrift, in hostile waters.

> 'Could be a lubrication problem' [the Petty Officer ERA had pronounced with professional detachment]. 'Might be something else tho! Could have been from towing too fast. 15? 20 knots? you say? Well, of course, if you do that sort of thing, sir, you're asking for it aren't you? That tub's only built for $7\frac{1}{2}$ knots. That prop and shaft are wizzing round. Those bearings might stand up to 14 for a while. Over that no matter how well they're packed, something's bound to give. Has to!'

They talked. Could the propeller be locked out while still disconnected from the engine? Perhaps, but that might cause other problems and severe damage elsewhere. How about safeguarding the bearings? Not really; they were either well greased or not. Just make sure they were packed fully from the start. What if something went wrong? Could repairs be carried out? That depended. It might be possible to botch if not too much damage had taken place. It would take an ERA to do it and it might be beyond him.

That was how it came about that when the draft plan was submitted to ACOS and passed to COHQ, a naval rating supplied by NOIC Lerwick had been added to the Assault Force, one whose qualifications would be Motor Mechanic. Exactly how Petty Officer Alfred Roe came to get the job is not so clear. The nomination would have had to be processed and approved by the Naval Officer in Command and to satisfy the important qualification that the rating concerned should be good at improvisation and knowledgeable of the relatively simple coble's machinery. It was also desirable that he should be a volunteer—as no doubt Roe was, although to what extent he acceded through self-respect (as opposed to genuine enthusiasm) to the suggestion that he might like to join a dangerous mission is open to speculation. Aged 36, Roe was a Londoner, the old man of the party, in good physical trim but, quite naturally, not at the peak of fitness attained by the others. It had come as a shock to fall into the hands of Jack Cox, but he survived with credit—and always in the hope that, in accordance with Godwin's intentions, he would remain sedentary, with the coble throughout and thus shielded from strenuous and prolonged physical strain or indulgence in military fisticuffs.

The plan submitted by ACOS and which passed the scrutiny of the Raiding Committee at COHQ was peculiary tentative. Intended as 'an attack on shipping in anchorages at Haugesund', it postulated delivering the coble by MTB in the approaches to the Skudenes Fjord and establishing an observation post on high ground on the north coast of the island of Vestre Bokn, where excellent views of the Karmsund and anchorages to the south of Haugesund, including those off Kopervik, could be obtained. Unfortunately, the latest intelligence stated that, of late, shipping had ceased to anchor there so much as in the past. It tended, instead, to stop to the north of Haugesund. So when Colonel Robert Neville of the Royal Marines, who was Mountbatten's Chief Coordinating Planner, came to study the plan prior to submitting it to his chief for approval, he expressed reservations about a scheme which, to some extent, related to a rather unimpressive meeting with Godwin. For as so often when in the presence of a dominant senior officer, Godwin entered his shell.

Robert Neville had played a leading part in the launching of the highly successful Operation FRANKTON, the raid by Royal Marine canoeists against shipping at Bordeaux. 'We did some pretty mad things', he admitted. 'None of us had any experience of this sort of thing. We were as ignorant as those we led. FRANKTON encouraged us but the irregulars were really blind.' For these reasons Neville was both interested by CHECKMATE—'a promising little operation'—and sceptical. But in commenting upon it he had to take into account Mountbatten's known willingness 'not to be over careful of chaps lives, and his dislike of wasteful effort and waste of of lives'. Also they were all under terrible pressure of work at COHQ where raiding was but one facet, a decreasing one, of their total effort. At that moment, in addition to several raids, large and small, projected into the near and distant future, they were deeply embroiled in a reorganisation of amphibious forces. Above all there was intensive planning of an invasion of Sicily, among other places in the Mediterranean, and consideration of major 'spoof' operations in North-west Europe to distract enemy attention from the real intended thrust line. Only limited time and attention could be given to a pinprick like CHECKMATE.

Due consideration had to be given to the politics of Godwin's project which in the final analysis was a naval occasion, backed by an Admiral, affecting naval strategy in sensitive Norwegian waters. Even by setting aside the Norwegian complications, Mountbatten was hardly likely to turn up his nose when asked by the Navy to carry out an operation with naval personnel in naval craft against naval targets. Usually it was the Admiralty or Admirals who applied the veto. When the boot was on the other foot, COHQ could not logically object.

Nevertheless, in discussion with Mountbatten and with the daily after-lunch Planning Coordinating Committee, Neville implied that, in recommending

CHECKMATE for implementation, he had reservations. That there was an inconsistency in proposing initially to attack shipping at Kovervik, when intelligence indicated it more frequently lay to the north at Haugesund, and merely stating that 'if shipping is in Haugesund an alternative plan will be required'.

> 'In other words' [he claimed] 'the main plan is produced for what is stated to be the most unlikely condition, and a very lightly sketched alternative plan for what is stated to be the most likely condition. I do not suggest that the alternative plan for the attack on Haugesund is by any means impossible, but it is plainly considerably more difficult.'

Having unburdened himself of those substantial worries, Neville went on to bow to ACOS's and Godwin's wishes.

> 'It seems we might almost just as well deposit Godwin and his crew in their hideout and set them to get on with it.'

With that Mountbatten and the Committee concurred, although Neville was careful to ensure, in his letter to ACOS of 19 April authorising CHECKMATE, that Vice Admiral Wells took his fair share of responsibility for the deed.

> 'The hours of darkness available' [he wrote] 'make the operation more hazardous than would have been the case had it been possible to carry it out a month ago. If you consider, however, that from the Naval approach point of view the short hours of darkness can be accepted, I request that this operation be mounted.'

And finally, to a drill frequently adopted for raids of this nature:

> 'It is not intended to issue any communiqué concerning the result to the Press, unless special circumstances arise when the point will be reconsidered.'

The 'suitable dates' for mounting remained set at between 23 April and 2 May, in the final moon phases. The detailed plan now drawn up by Job and Godwin for ACOS's signature remained substantially as originally conceived except for a few vital changes.

Still, at this late stage, no suitable radio operator had been found. Besides, the bulky set and heavy batteries provided were found to overload the coble, the much lighter and more compact set issued to SOE parties apparently being unsuitable. In any case, wiser counsels had prevailed over the uses for which the set was intended. For fear of location by enemy direction finding, it would not be used to report success and signalling to the pick-up MTB would now be in accordance to a fixed schedule. As finally settled, the MTB would call at the Urter islands, off the north coast of Karmøy, on D + 11, failing that D + 18, with contact from ship to shore by 'special torches'.

The dropping of the radio operator and his set provided Godwin with a welcome opportunity to strengthen his team and for Sergeant Cox to take his chance. Hard as he had been upon them all, they had come to appreciate his value. They respected the thoroughness of his infantryman's skill; his happy knack of somehow making them laugh, as martyrs should, at the trials thrust upon them; and the manner in which he shared the rigours he enforced, never asking them to do something he could not. And the way he cheerfully let them have their revenge by submitting to a crash course in canoeing, taking the duckings they inflicted upon him as just retribution. Between Cox and the sailors there developed a special dialogue, a mixture of Army Commando and Royal Navy jargon, slang and repartée as offshoots of a fierce pride which determined that neither Service's representatives should score points over the other. Additionally, Godwin had realised that Cox's previous employment as a lorry driver might be useful back-up for Petty Officer Motor Mechanic Alfred Roe. But essentially Cox won the place he coveted because he had made himself one of them with a vital contribution to make.

After discussion with Job, Godwin settled upon 29 April as D-Day. In the week between receipt of the COHQ authorisation and the moment Godwin could tell his crew to prepare themselves for action, under the guise of another exercise, last-minute preparations were merged with routine training. In fact they all guessed the real thing was not far off, and welcomed it, as a tingling of nervous expectation took flight from natural dread of the unexpected.

Discussion periods and quizzes to test their knowledge assumed real significance. Now that the coble crew had been strengthened by the inclusion of Roe and Cox under Hiscock, as Coxswain, the canoeists Ordinary Seamen West, Mayor and Burgess felt a lot more secure. Certainly Hiscock was glad to have companions to share the watches and strengthen his shore defences in the hide. For the older men—Roe, Hiscock and Cox—the strain was greater than for the youngsters, whose imaginations did not stretch as far as their elders and to whom the dangers involved were more remote. Not that any of them, with the possible exception of Roe, really imagined anything could go wrong. 'It can't happen to me' was the prevalent attitude. But the elders thought more deeply and Roe was bound to worry about the wife who awaited him and who had not the slightest idea he was not still safe in a comfortable job ashore.

Without admitting to the possibility of failure, they listened patiently to the routine lectures about security, escape and evasion. They reheard the old chestnuts of supplying 'Name, Rank and Number' in accordance with the rules of war if captured; of the duty to conceal from the enemy anything liable to be of use to him by way of information; the duty to escape and to do so at the first opportunity when it might be easier than later from within the prison camp. Also about the latest situation within Norway—the extent to which they might receive help from the people if they were on the run; the danger of betrayal by the handful of Quislings; how to survive in the wild if they struck out across the mountains for Sweden, remembering that in the south the population was denser and the problems of steering clear of trouble, in some respects, harder than in the wilder north. But although they paid attention to the representatives from M19 in the War Office and also to the doctor giving a repeat performance of his First Aid lectures—the staunching of bleeding and treatment of wounds and burns, etc.—their minds fixed chiefly upon the job in hand—mixed with speculation as to where it might be, and when.

10

Landfall

There had been no sense of impending disaster when Godwin and his crew went aboard the coble at last light on 28 April. Just a feeling of relief that at last they were on their way. Fynn, Waggett and Job had come to see them off and wish them well. They settled down, nursing their weapons as 'Trilby' Roe (now known by a nickname) started the engine and Shorty Hiscock took the helm. There had been subdued cheers from coble to shore as they headed for the south entrance to the harbour, secure in the knowledge that the weather forecast was good.

A few minutes later, at 0015 B, MTB 626, under command of Lieutenant Knut Bøgeberg, had slipped and proceeded to make rendezvous with the coble and, at 0030 B, make fast the tow. With practised ease the commandos handed up their weapons to Børresen and his reception party on deck and clambered aboard, bringing the few items of personal kit they might require on passage. Up on the bridge Bøgeberg welcomed Godwin as the men settled in below. Fifteen minutes after coming alongside the big engines opened up. In a light breeze, with a calm sea and good visibility, they had set course at 15 knots on a bearing calculated to mislead prying eyes as to their true destination.

It was an uneventful voyage without suspicion of another craft, friend or foe. Midway across Godwin called a conference in a secluded corner to announce, what they already assumed, that this was the real thing, and to explain the plan. On the chart they saw for the first time the Karmsund and Haugesund, along with symbols denoting the numerous enemy watch posts and defences. They heard, too, the outline plan approved by COHQ and issued by ACOS. Godwin told them no more than was necessary to help them take an intelligent part in the raid and be able to extemporise if the need arose when they were on their own. He was careful, of course, to omit such vital information as the position of the intended first hide and the observation post high on the Boknafjell, or the islands where the MTB would find them for pick-up. It was a risk to keep them in ignorance. Suppose he was killed? What of them? Yet he had also to bear in mind that if any one of them fell into enemy hands and was in a position under pressure to divulge such information, it might go ill for others. It was a golden rule never to jeopardise comrades or valuable equipment. For that same reason, Bøgeberg alone among his crew knew the exact place where to drop Godwin and not the slightest hint of the pick-up point or, indeed, that he might later have to do that job in MTB 626.

Also for security reasons Godwin rubbed in again the importance of steering clear of Norwegians ashore.

'The first hide out is selected for its loneliness on Vestre Bokn and its nearness to a good observation post. There's hardly a soul about—except probably a few fishermen. But they can be a menace! They don't miss a thing. Still, with any luck we'll be tucked away snug before first light and they won't spot us. The coble's a lot easier to camouflage than a darned great MTB.'

Water creaming up from her bow and spray occasionally driving across the bridge as, engines humming, she sheered the grey sea, MTB 626 held course several points to northward of the planned drop-off point at the entrance to the Skudenes Fjord. Behind streamed the coble, riding comfortably on the turbulence of the MTB's wake, dipping her beautifully raked bow only when Bøgeberg experimented with a short burst at 20 knots. Something to do with the towing attachment, he reckoned. He would sort that out before next time. Some of the time Godwin spent on the bridge, studying the coble, chatting to his hosts and satisfying himself that nothing was being done to jeopardise the mission. He looked thoughtful and extremely observant, taking his share in watching for the slightest indication that they might have been spotted by the enemy, from sea or air. When darkness began to enshroud them, some 70 miles off the coast, nothing had been spotted—they hoped. Reasonably satisfied, he went below to join the others, report all well, and take a meal before making the final preparations.

By the faint light of the northern glow, Bøgeberg altered course at 2217 B hrs towards the Utsira Islands off Karmøy, and made an accurate landfall at 0015 B hrs, D + 1, 30 April. Slightly envious of the Norwegian's proficiency in navigating with such precise artistry, Godwin monitored the craft's course to southward, listening to the commentary among officers as they checked off silhouetted features ashore against the chart, realising, too, that one or two among the crew had also already recognised exactly where they were. In a heavy swell, exactly at 0130 B, Bøgeberg ordered engines stopped and announced to his passenger:

'This is it. That's Geitungen over there. Five miles off at 240°.'

He pointed to the southmost tip of Karmøy, a small island which in happier days would have been visible by a lighthouse's repeated flashing.

'And that's Kvitisøy, over there' [pointing to starboard]. 'So here we are, John. On time, at the entrance to the Skudeness Fjord which, I am afraid is behaving badly, as it usually does when the wind's in this quarter. Are you ready?'

Clad in khaki oilskins over battledress, Godwin's crew lined the rail, weapons in hand. The heavy swell made transfer to the coble extremely difficult as the two craft plunged up and down against each other and the sailors were hard-pressed to fend off and prevent damage. Eventually it took 30 minutes — far longer than expected, thus reducing the time available to travel in-shore and find a suitable hide, perhaps even preventing them from reaching the northern end of Vestre Bokn as planned.

> '0200 B: Coble proceeded. MTB 626 proceeded to seaward at slow speed, waiting in case coble should get into difficulty.'

This was the moment of truth, the last chance for Godwin to withdraw from the deliberately taken gamble at the coble's capacity to withstand so long and testing a voyage at excessive speed. Often he had let imagination focus on the screw, its shaft rotating madly within frail bearings at a speed far in excess of that for which they had been designed. As a precaution, he had asked Bøgeberg to stay on hand just in case, at the last moment, something was found wrong. With Hiscock at the tiller and Roe engaging the drive, the Petty Officer Motor Mechanic, Godwin and Cox had their ears finely tuned to detect the slightest rumble of failure.

To Børresen:

> 'The spirit of the men was on top when we left them. They were smiling and waving as if they were just going ashore to turn a switch and stop the war.'

Of course, it was hardly likely that, before the much respected Norwegians, they would do otherwise. Pride was as much a nationalistic impulse as the Service and unit one.

For Bøgeberg it was an anxious interlude in which he held on to the last moment, at risk of his boat, in case a signal of distress was received. His attention switched from clock to coble, thence to the approaching enemy coast and then back to the clock, calculating how much longer he could delay the high-speed dash for safety before daylight. But after 30 minutes all seemed normal. With a last cheery wave to Godwin, who put up his thumbs, he ordered 23 knots for home, to tie up at Lerwick 23 hours later and report the CHECKMATE party well and truly launched on its mission.

Launched Godwin and his men most assuredly were. But not so well and truly. The MTB was barely out of sight before the propeller transmission began to vibrate and make unwelcome noises. Hardly waiting for Godwin's order, Roe pushed the gear lever into neutral and began an examination of the shaft with its two bearings housed in a tunnel. As he ruefully expected, both bearings were red hot and by his judgement seriously damaged. Until they cooled down, he advised Godwin, the engine should not be used, otherwise the bearings, if they had not already 'run' beyond repair, would be a total write-off. Better, in fact, that they should be left alone completely until he had stripped them down ashore to discover the full extent of the harm. He was not very optimistic though.

Hiscock and the others listened and watched in anxious silence as Godwin sat deep in thought. By his estimate at that crucial moment they lay some five miles from the southernmost cape of Vestre Bokn, although little less than a mile off Karmøy, which was clearly visible in the moonlight. A less resolute person might justifiably and prudently have cut his losses and made there and then for the nearest haven, hoping even in the fairly densely populated territory in the vicinity of Skudeneshavn to elude detection. They might even then repair the coble and yet pursue their mission. If not, nobody would criticise him for doing so—except himself. Pride warped his assessment and planning; self-respect and an unwillingness to admit failure and return, once more, from an abortive mission in the CRACKERS manner, steered his course. On a rough calculation, he reckoned that by alternatively paddling the coble and employing short bursts of engine power, after the bearings and shaft had cooled, they should reach the southern tip of Vestre Bokn shortly before daylight.

They began to paddle, lunging with the small, single canoe blades and taking it in turn, two a side. It was hard labour, the heavy coble dead in the water and an awkward brute for men to drive from inefficient positions across the gunwales. The best speed against a cross-current was one knot—and that condemned them to exposure in hostile waters in full daylight, prey to the first enemy patrol boat to happen along in what, normally, was a fairly busy channel. At the first attempt to run the engine at slow speed it was almost immediately obvious that the mere cooling of the bearings was insufficient. The expensive sounding noises at once returned. Emphatically Roe again protested that to continue must wreak irreparable damage. So it was back to the paddles with renewed desperation and an all-too-slow rate of progress towards the misty outline of Vestre Bokn in the moonlight.

When the glimmer of dawn appeared they were still nearly two miles adrift, but fortunately, as yet, alone in the mouth of the Karmsund. Slowly—far too slowly—they began to narrow the distance to the nearest islet which the chart named Busholmane. From the tiller Hiscock called attention to something ashore which did not quite match with the otherwise even panorama of sandy coloured foreshore, rocks and dark scrub.

'People moving about among those buildings' [he said].

'OK, Coxs'n' [acknowledged Godwin who guessed at once what it probably was] 'but don't start pointing and none of the rest of you look interested. Just keep paddling. That's a German battery over there. The one the Intelligence people call the Klepp battery.'

They pulled all the harder, striving might and main to round the point while Godwin crouched low over the gunwale to examine the enemy through binoculars.

'Keep going' [he urged them]. 'They're too busy to worry about us at present. It's the morning gun cleaning parade. They're all pushing and shoving with cleaning rods which probably means too that the breaches are all stripped down.'

Now was the time to find out if the coble and its crew would pass inspection as Norwegian. He removed his officer's peaked cap and had the others stow away their distinctive headgear too, except for Cox, who thought he looked just the part of a fisherman in his Army issue knitted 'cap comforter'. At any moment they expected to see the Germans leaping to their guns or a patrol boat coming to intercept. An eternity elapsed before, sweating and heaving (but without appearing to be in panic), they placed the headland between themselves and the battery, remarked upon by somebody with the words, 'If Jerry hasn't got us now, he never will.' Escape contributed a much wanted uplift, one which was only partly undermined when, somewhat fatigued, they closed on Busholmane, the first island in sight, to discover that as a refuge it was rather small and none too well covered.

Godwin declined to go farther. Choosing a tiny inlet at the corner most distant from the Klepp battery, he had them rapidly throw nets over the coble while he and Cox reconnoitred to settle upon an observation post and defence plan. Only then did he let them begin the preparation of a meal and allow Roe to start an investigation of the machinery. It did not take Roe long to establish the extent of the damage. It was bad. Perhaps beyond repair without completely new bearings and, maybe, a new shaft. He might be able to botch it up for a short journey, he told Godwin. But it would not last. That long voyage with the propeller dragging round the shaft at high revolutions had caused ruination, a disaster which, as Godwin realised, had further reaching consequences than a mere mechanical breakdown.

With the failure of his gamble upon the durability of the coble, his entire plan of campaign was in disarray. Already well behind schedule and far short of his initial destination at the northern end of Vestre Bokn, he was also deprived of the mobile base upon which his strategy depended. To make matters worse, he was sitting right under the enemy's nose without the slightest notion of what to do next. He needed time to think. Yet even this was denied him when West attracted his attention to a signal from Burgess, who was on watch, pointing to seaward where already a small motor boat was approaching.

Osvald and Reidar Pederson were out fishing from Kopervik and within sight of Busholmane when one of them noticed that there was something special and strange about the familiar island. Since April 1940 the flotsam and jetsam of war had frequently been washed up, along with the bodies of sailors and airmen. Fishermen had become accustomed to investigating anything unusual. To be confronted by men pointing sten guns at them was, however, unique in the Pedersons's experience, but then to be invited ashore to share cigarettes and chocolate reassuring. They realised, of course, the danger of fraternisation without at once grasping that Godwin's hospitality was in emulation of Charles Herlofson's ploy to compromise Norwegians and irrevocably enmesh them in the action. Not that this deterred the Pedersons from offering help when it was explained to them that the boat had mechanical trouble and that assistance was needed—an indication how, already, Roe was unsure of being able to make repairs. They said they would do what they could, and set off for Kopervik to consult a man who owned larger fishing boats and whom they knew was no Quisling.

As they left, the full implications of the meeting was born upon Godwin. Within minutes of touching Norwegian soil he was not only involved with the populace but begging them for assistance right under the enemy's noses. Giving instructions to improve the coble's concealment, he settled down to reconsider the plan. The initial thoughts which had deterred him from abandoning the mission off Skudeneshavn prevailed. Somehow he would persevere and sink a ship or two by use of the canoes alone, since the coble was permanently incapacitated. Measuring distances on the chart, he reckoned it possible to paddle the nine miles separating him from Kopervik in the space of a night—providing no enemy interference or inclement weather conditions were encountered in the guarded and yet exposed Karmsund. He was working upon the reallocation of stores between the marooned coble and the two canoes when the second visitor arrived.

Erling Jøssang was inspecting his lobster pots when, like the Pedersons, he detected the coble shrouded none too effectively under its net and, upon investigating, also found himself looking down a gun barrel at short range. With him, the Herlofson treatment was every bit as compromising as with the earlier callers, although with difficulty due to the language problem. Unlike the Pedersons, Jøssang could speak virtually no English. Nevertheless, with phrases in German, some astute phonetic interpretation by West and Burgess (the two Northerners whose accents most closely approximated to Norwegian) and articulate sign language, conversation was possible.

Three years of German invigilance had taught Jøssang not to ask questions.

But, pointing with powerful gestures to the chart and then to the sea, he managed to convey the impression that their refuge was wide open to combinations of strong, prevailing winds and currents, a death trap made all the more insecure by the close proximity of the Klepp battery and by frequent surveillance from inquisitive patrol boats. The sooner they were elsewhere the better, and he, Erling Jøssang, was the guide they needed to pilot them that night to a safer spot. He was most insistent and overcame Godwin's ingrained misgivings because, as Godwin had to admit to himself, there really was no other choice.

Before Jøssang's boat reappeared that evening, Godwin had finalised and explained his revised plan to the crew. He and the three Ordinary Seamen in the canoes would press on with the original intention. That night, leaving behind the coble, with Hiscock, Roe and Cox, the canoe party would go through the narrow sheltered channel dividing Vestre from Austre Bokn to a hide on the island of Føsenoy, opposite Kopervik. Compared with the shorter route up the Karmsund, with its hazards of rougher water and strong enemy defences, he guessed the longer way round might be quicker. There were penalties, of course. They would have to live rough, dispensing with tents and braving the elements, which could be fractious at this time, although so far kind. To carry more food they would have to reduce the number of limpets to four per canoe, just enough for two ships if they were lucky enough to find them. And they would not have much time to spare. It was now 30 April. They ought to be back at Busholmane by 4 May if they were to be sure of meeting the MTB on the 9th.

As for the coble — he would take a chance and trust this man Jøssang to find them a new hide and not give them away. It seemed a reasonable risk. So, as soon as the tide had receded, Roe was to patch up the bearings as best he could for the short trip that night and try to do a more permanent job while the canoes were away. Good enough to carry them the twenty-odd miles to the pick-up point when required.

They listened intently, gauging imponderables and coming face-to-face with their predicament when their officer moved on to outline action in the worst possible case should everything fall apart. This time there was no joking over evasion and escape procedures. The likelihood of their necessity had become all too plain. Godwin instructed that, should the canoes fail to get back to the coble by the 5th, Hiscock, with Roe and Cox, was to make for Urter where the MTB would pick them up on the night of 9/10 May, or a week later if that failed. Originally, Godwin had intended to withold that item for security reasons; now it was no longer justifiable to do so. A lot would depend upon the weather, he knew, and upon Roe's success with the coble. If Urter seemed beyond reach, they should make for the mainland in the last resort and try to reach Sweden, overland. They knew the problems. It would be hard going and difficult to evade the Germans and the Quislings in a land whose people lived in torment and whose language they did not speak. But they should try if only for their own good. Capture threatened such dire consequences.

This led to the cover plan he had formulated in case they were caught and interrogated. They all knew that if the Germans really put their minds to it, resistance to coercion and torture—and they had the latter in mind—could not be withstood for long. In certain circumstances, Godwin said, there was something to be said for appearing fairly co-operative and saying what they had been up to, just so long as vital information was witheld. By that he meant witholding information concerning future operations (of which, in any case, they knew virtually nothing) and matters relating to the safety of others—above all the MTB crews and those Norwegians who had helped them. It was vital to conceal the time and place of pick-up.

'Just stick to a yarn that the MTB didn't turn up and that you were going to pinch a fishing boat to get home. If the Jerrys get the slightest hint that Urter is the RV the boys from 30th Flotilla will be for it. And if we don't get back together again, let them think you're on your own. Don't mention the other party. The longer Jerry's kept guessing the better for us all. And finally don't trust the Norwegians any more than you have to. This chap Jøssang looks OK. But you can't be sure. He might be playing a double game and you can never tell what the Germans might do to him or his people if they smell a rat. At the same time, for God's sake don't let on about what he or anybody else has done for us. Jøssang and people like him won't thank you if you do. They'll be for the chop, particularly if we manage to do what we mean to do before it's all over.'

They spent an hour or more mulling the situation over, cross-checking details, reallocating stores, speculating about eventualities and the cover plan, making suggestions and pooling ideas. This was when the freemasonry Godwin had encouraged over the months proved so useful. Nobody, not even the youngest member, Porky Burgess, felt in the least inhibited about express-ing an opinion or contributing to the plan. Before the session was over Godwin had managed to lift their hopes by ejecting a trickle of pessimism with the flood of his own optimism in the thrall of scheming for a bright outcome. He had them believing again in their salvation through aggressive action—which was something of a personal feat, since he was all too aware of his own responsibility for their plight. No doubt he had his own morale in mind when he rounded off the session by indulging in exortation.

'What I am asking of you is well within our strength and capacity. Twelve miles paddling in one spell we've done before—and more. We can lick that side of it even if the weather turns nasty. West and I coped with far worse in Sognefjord last month than we're likely to suffer here.

It comes down to survival really. Never let up. Remember what Sergeant Cox has banged in. Commandos don't shrug their shoulders and say "sod it" and if the Commandos can do that, so can the Royal Navy. We're in this war for King and Country. You fight for all your worth for that, and for the rest of us and for your people at home. Just remember that.'

11

Attack

When Erling Jøssang came back to Busholmane shortly after nightfall it was to find the British party packed up and ready to go. He piloted them northwards into a large bay in the direction of Hognaland until they came in less than a mile to the rocky island of Kjeøyna. Here in a narrow passage between cliffs they hid the coble, piling seaweed upon it so that, as Jøssang remarked with satisfaction, 'you had to lay your hands on the boat to discover it'. Past midnight, he left them, followed shortly, at a discreet distance, by Godwin, West, Mayor and Burgess in their canoes, leaving Hiscock, Roe and Cox to work on the coble and sweat it out.

Undoubtedly it came as a relief to Godwin to settle to hard paddling in the canoe, a way of relieving the tensions of anguish and frustration by solid manual labour directed at the original goal. It was impossible, of course, to erase absolutely the problem of the marooned coble crew and the danger in which they all stood. But there was satisfaction in maintaining the momentum of CHECKMATE with intent to strike a blow, however reduced, against the enemy. Contentedly he matched the powerful Andrew West's rate of striking, the paddles rising and dipping like windmill sails as they swept through enticingly slack waters which reminded him of the days spent training in Scotland's enclosed lochs and firths. With unbroken rhythm, the two canoes in close station with each other, they followed the shore of Vestre Bokn, heading for the Boknasund which offered even smoother water. Austre Bokn lay to starboard. To port rose up the imposing slopes of the Boknafjell, majestic in the moonlight—a wonderful observation post if only the coble had not let them down and the original plan had remained intact. Progress remained good, quite uninterrupted by any need to take evasive action against a hostile presence. Navigation in moonlight was also easy with so many prominent landmarks in sight. But as they swung westward towards Hallvardsvig it became obvious that, with dawn almost upon them, they must abandon what little hope they had of entering the Karmsund in darkness. The time lost in moving and hiding the coble had now to be paid for, making them, as they searched for a suitable hide near Hallvardsvig, at least 24 hours behind the original schedule.

If only they had been able that night to paddle the two or three miles still separating them from Kopervik, it would have saved them a full 18 hours' indolence with nothing to do but sleep and stand guard against unlucky discovery by Norwegians or an enemy patrol. Now, instead of being able, as intended, to spend four or five days lurking with the coble, they would have available little more than 24 hours confined to the attack area with the chances of finding a target commensurately reduced. It was extremely galling! Impatiently they left Hallvardsvig next night, heading west to pick up the navigation lights marking the entrance to the Austdjup and almost immediately seeing, spread out before them, the Karmsund and the dark mass of Karmøy beyond.

The realisation they were re-entering guarded waters in no way discouraged them, even though the initial 'plain sailing' attitude now had to be replaced by the hunter's guile. Staying close to the dark shore of Fosenøy, which Intelligence had reported as bare of enemy positions, they automatically obtained protection in the shadows from the profusion of artillery and machine-gun emplacements surrounding Kopervik, less than a mile distant. By courtesy of the beacon lights, they were able to steer confidently, heading for the beacon at Dua, where, Godwin judged from the chart, a good view of the entire port and anchorage of Kopervik could be had. So well did they progress, with time to spare, that Godwin even toyed with the wild idea of trying to mine a ship that night if one should happen to be anchored nearby.

That was only a rogue impulse, snuffed out by the emptiness of the sund and a second thought governed by the small voice telling him that patience was a virtue, even in wartime. Finding a hide took first priority and proved simple. There were several small inlets with thick cover among rocks or vegetation not far from the shoreline. Moreover, the canoes' light weight made it possible to lift them, along with their loads, a short distance from the water's edge, out of sight and reach of inevitable fishermen. They selected an ideal spot—close to the water, easily concealed among evergreens and with all-round observation plus shelter from the weather should it deteriorate. From frequent practice, they quickly settled down while Mayor and Burgess began to prepare a meal on the hexamine stoves and, as the light improved, Godwin and West took the first watch.

2 May, of necessity, had to be a day of hiding, watching and waiting—with the enticement of action that night. It was work demanding the utmost caution, since the slightest false movement might betray their position. Carefully hidden among the long grass and with faces blackened, they were extremely difficult to detect. Yet a mere flicker of reflection from binoculars, or an unwary twitch when changing position or effecting a relief between watches, might catch the eye of an alert observer, be he friend or foe. As Godwin appreciated, these conditions were quite unlike those at the Sognefjord. There the enemy was at a distance, a few dots on the landscape. Here they were close in large numbers, recognisable on passing craft and where they

stood duty in the emplacements protecting Kopervik. Quite soon Godwin noticed that Mayor and Burgess, to whom the disciplines of watching were new, tended to be slightly offhand. For that reason he changed the pairing, swapping Mayor for West, so that the latter, to whom watching was familiar business, could supervise Burgess.

Throughout the day a pattern of military and civilian behaviour in the area became noticeable. Patrol boats passed irregularly, but seemed mainly intent upon examining the Norwegian fishing boats which came and went in their usual numbers. Only occasionally did anybody bother to spare more than a glance for the shore. As for the sentry who changed post every two hours on the 45-mm gun position situated on the headland to the north of Kopervik, his attitude looked more like one of boredom enlivened by keen alertness when the guard commander or an officer happened along. Why should he do otherwise? Who was likely to play tricks in broad daylight where no tricks had been played before?

Once Godwin had located and related to the map the exact position of each enemy post, he began to identify lines of approach and formulate alternative schemes for attacking targets wherever they happened to offer themselves. Naturally he concentrated at first upon the likely anchorages outside the small harbour of Kopervik. But as the day wore on and nothing anchored—indeed not one ship passed—he turned his attention to the harbour itself, studying a coaling wharf with its crane to the north and the commercial quay with its painted wooden warehouses nestling on the southern bank of the main inlet. Plainly no vessel much above 1000 tons was likely to berth there. All that was to be seen at present was a coaster, several fishing boats moored around her, and, towards evening, a trawler of about 300 tons which flew the ensign of the German Navy and was fitted with minesweeping gear. Neither, in his judgement, was worth the risk and turmoil of sinking. By nightfall, indeed, the predictions of the Intelligence people had been realised. All too obviously shipping was no longer anchoring at this spot.

The dilemma was hard to resolve. To remain longer, a further 24 hours, was to risk being late for the rendezvous with the coble. That might have untold effects upon its crew's composure. He had also to take into account the weather, which, having been kind so far, might soon break. A high respect for the viciousness of the Norwegian climate in these waters had been hard won on CRACKERS. But to abandon the operation without striking a blow, as they had abandoned CRACKERS, seemed unthinkable. The conflict of emotions within him was painful, transmitted by inflections to his companions who waited trustingly for him to make up his mind—partly willing, if the truth be known, that perhaps they should take a chance and stay another day, in the Micawberish hope of something turning up; partly grasping the opinion that if fate was against them they should not push their luck! Yet they had enough confidence in their stamina and ability with canoes to believe they could afford to waste another day, still carry out an attack and yet get back to the coble and the MTB pick-up, even if the weather cracked. Thus had the hardening of the commando process, honed by Cox, put a fierce cutting edge upon their resolve.

Godwin, however, had gambled once upon the coble and lost. He was not prepared to redouble the risk to the lives of his men—and himself—by gambling again. He would limit the risks by tackling the only available target that night, within Kopervik, even though that meant running the gauntlet of defences which were infinitely stronger than the outposts he had met at the Sognefjord. Here, in a manner of speaking by comparison, were ramparts with interlocking fields of fire designed to repel an invasion by strong forces, not a mere sub-lieutenant and three ordinary seamen armed with sten guns, vulnerably exposed in paper-thin canoes. And yet it was the very impudence of their impending raid which attracted him. Recalling a song by Stanley Holloway, he felt a little bit like the child who 'poked his stick with the 'orse's 'ead 'andle' into the lion's ear—except that he intended not to be eaten up 'ole as a result.

> 'We'll have a go to-night' [he told the others]. 'I refuse to leave without posting our calling card. I know its a rotten little ship and hardly worth the bother, but that minesweeper over there's all there is. We'll take her to-night. Then scram before the rumpus begins.'

He outlined the plan and had them eat before throwing the camouflage off the canoes, restowing and carrying them to the water's edge ready for launching. Shortly before midnight, with sufficient moonlight to see and without need to map read, they were striking out for the opposite bank.

It would be fatuous to suggest that each in his own way did not suffer from a typical, scared tightening of the muscles, a slight loosening of the bowels or minor palpitations when the moment of realisation arrived. Fear of the enemy and the unknown are potent fermentors of tensions. So too is the thrill of at last carrying out what they had long intended plus the satisfaction of putting into practice an unproven theory. In a way this was the first night of a play they had dress rehearsed so successfully at Lerwick a month ago. Though nobody, not even Godwin with his theatrical talent, gave a second's thought to the logical inversion of the old adage that a chaotic dress rehearsal might make all well on the first night—or, for that matter, much consideration to the loss of life they might cause.

They copied the Lerwick drill, crossing the Karmsund in close company by the shortest route to a point near Byggnes where the defences were thinnest, guarded only by that single position to the north of Kopervik, pausing there for a few minutes to give the enemy a chance to reveal any suspicions. Then, since nothing stirred, commencing the approach to the harbour, paddling to pass beneath the headland so as to be obscured from the sentry's sight.

They hardly noticed the coal wharf so intent were they upon their objective — the miniature forest of masts and smoke stacks belonging to the fishing boats and the coasters, huddled two to three abreast at the quay's inner end, with the minesweeper tied up at the outer pier, closest to the Karmsund. In its simplicity the implementation of Godwin's plan was incredibly reminiscent of that night attack on the destroyer in Lerwick a month ago. Here, once more, were shaded lights, deep shadows, rippled water and the hum of ship's machinery. Only sounds of roistering ashore were missing. In accordance with the set procedure, they stopped to swap double for single paddles and exchange final, whispered sentences, almost, but not precisely, the same way as at Lerwick. Godwin again told Mayor to hang back and make his attempt only if it was obvious that the first try had failed — but pointing out now, as further insurance against error, the correct route to follow east and southward to a rendezvous beyond the harbour when the job was done. And this time, once Mayor had acknowledged with the customary 'Aye Aye, sir', he had leant across to shake his officer's hand as he said 'Good Luck'. And at that there had been handshakes all round — representing a cheer — before Godwin quietly told West to paddle.

Neither sign nor sound came from the wharf or decks as they closed the ships, although Godwin assumed somebody would be on watch and, presumably, awake. They glided close by the fishing boats, feeling pretty safe that their crews would be ashore or asleep, and silently, from out of the shadows, emerged under their victim's stern. Here Godwin selected a limpet and turned the priming key, sighing with relief when he confirmed, what previously he had judged only though binoculars, that the hull was of metal construction. No fiddling around with screw limpets, thank God! Already, without prompting, Andrew West was back-paddling to station the canoe, broadside on, exactly 6 feet from the minesweeper's side, in readiness for Godwin to hook the limpet to the pole, swing it out and make contact. This time there was no fiddling around as at Lerwick, despite slight muscular tremors born of excitement. This time, too, the magnets gripped first shot. At the sight of the pole detaching and swinging, unladen, West eased forward the precise distance in readiness for the second placement. And so far not a sound from above on deck.

Systematically, without a trace of over-confidence, they fixed all four as fears of discovery progressively were dismissed from their minds. With professional concentration they completed the job within less than five minutes and unhurriedly slipped sundwards beyond the ship's bows — and into the arcs of fire of the invisible but as yet silent machine-gun positions. And at that moment of triumph, when it all seemed in the bag, the alarm sounded.

Never was Keith Mayor satisfactorily to explain why or how it was that he allowed his canoe to come within sight of the minesweeper. It was not an attempt on his part to make a solo attack, since he was perfectly capable of estimating how long must pass before he could be sure Godwin had failed.

More likely, he thought, he had momentarily lost concentration upon station keeping, so anxious was he for Godwin and West, and in so doing had permitted the canoe to drift off station with the tide. Or perhaps he had become disorientated by the shadows. Whatever the reason, the first he and Burgess knew of being near enough to the minesweeper was for somebody on deck to spot them. There was the sound of running feet, a shout of 'Achtung ein boat', followed by a rush of sailors to the rail to gaze at an indistinct dark shape off the beam. To their credit, Godwin and West kept their heads perfectly, abstaining from the assumption that it was they who had been spotted and remaining motionless, heads down in their seats while the canoe's existing momentum carried her away. Also, to the credit of Mayor and Burgess, they too refrained from panic as they paddled without haste, as of a casual outing, praying the Germans would take them for Norwegians on some illicit midnight jaunt.

It was a bad moment, bringing home to them all, perhaps for the first time in its entirety, the uncertainties of a saboteur's mission. Yet, unexpectedly as the alarm had been when given, as rapidly did its fuss die away. Nothing happened and therefore it was two very relieved crews which converged a few minutes later, beyond the harbour, hardly believing their luck. A single shot from the ship would have been enough to alert the machine-gun posts sited to sweep the eastern and southern approaches to the port, and little imagination required to apprehend searchlights' beams probing the darkness, flares arcing up and tracer bullets flickering and lashing the water around their canoes.

Little was said, except for Godwin to tell Mayor and Burgess that the job was done and that, in view of what had happened, they must clear off immediately. There was no question now of making a second attempt next day. When the mines detonated in four hours' time, all hell would be let loose and the Germans were sure to connect the explosions with the report of a nearby boat. It was out with double paddles and full steam ahead for the point at Fosenøy *en route* for the hide at Hallvardsvig. There to recuperate before, the following night, of 3/4 May, completing the expedition by returning to the coble and making plans for final departure.

It would be ridiculous to claim that John Godwin or his crew were satisfied by the result of their adventure. To come so far to sink a mere piddling little minesweeper—always assuming that the mines would function and that sunk she would be—was nothing to get excited about. Some might say it was a wasted effort—and an unjustified one, too, if next day an enraged enemy twigged what had happened and began hunting them seriously. Moreover, reflected Godwin, he now understood why Charles Herlofson had so low an opinion of laying mines without being able to see the fruits of his endeavours. From their hide on Vestre Bokn nothing could be seen of Kopervik and the sound of explosions would not carry the distance. Maybe they would never know what happened—although if, next day, the waters about them swarmed with searchers, joyous conclusions might be permissible.

But next day came and went without a hint of disturbance. Fishermen carried out their chores. Patrol boats were conspicuous by their absence. Life was idyllic—or might have been had not the weather broken with a rising wind from the south-west driving in cloud, rain and fog to the classic pattern of that region. How glad Godwin was that the coble was no longer exposed to these forces on the island of Busholmane. Hiscock and his companions could stay snug and safe and that night they would be reunited. All being well, too, Roe and Cox would have fixed the prop-shaft, enabling them to cruise at leisure to Urter and meet the MTB according to plan.

Basking in this warming shaft of optimism, Godwin could actually whip up sensations of self-congratulation, a feeling that, in resisting the temptation to push his luck any farther after, at least, making a mark upon the Germans, he had absolved himself from errors committed. Yet this very train of thought brought with it a fierce resolve to carry his men home. They were not yet out of the wood. So this was the moment to alter his aim from its concentration upon inflicting harm upon the enemy to one of preservation of life, the lives of his men and himself. How clearly this was formulated at this moment is open to doubt. Nevertheless, this was when he made a positive step in the new direction by ditching the remaining four limpets and thus renouncing all future offensive intention, at the same time marginally lightening the canoes upon whose speed their lives must now depend.

12

The Coble's Story

Unlike the closely-knit community of the canoe quartet, the coble's trio of occupants were a diverse bunch, their principal common denominator being that of age. They were the elders of the CHECKMATE party. In other respects, however, they also were unmatched among themselves in background, qualifications and experience so that when it came to tackling a specialist problem they could draw on a wide range of talents; but when it came to acquiring a unified approach they judged affairs by different standards and from separate viewpoints. There had to be divergences between the New-foundlander Hiscock, who was a past member of the Patrol Service and with involvement with war in Tobruk during the siege in 1942, and Cox the countryman trained as a killer but devoid of active service. And neither of these could possibly share the outlook of Roe, the married townsman technician who had joined the party partly out of default, and could not wholeheartedly share the vibrant volunteering enthusiasm of the others.

On 1 May (while Godwin and his party were in hiding at Hallvardsvig), Roe and Cox had begun dismantling the propeller shaft and its bearings while Hiscock kept watch. It came as no surprise when they laid bare the state of the shaft. Both had seen the ravages of severe under-lubrication and over-heating before and both knew that the only worthwhile solution was replacement of the damaged parts. But by moving from Busholmane to Kjeøyna they had cut themselves off from the Pedersons who had offered to provide the spares and help required. In reply to the question 'Can you fix it?'—meaning 'What are our chances of getting to Urter and home?'—Roe could only admit that they were slim. He would clean up the mess and pack the bearings with grease. But, especially if run at full power and maximum revolutions, as required to cope with strong currents or heavy seas, that would not last. Which meant, as Hiscock at once realised, that only in fair weather and smooth waters dare they risk navigating off the exposed coast of Karmøy *en route* to Urter. It also meant that, without the coble, somebody among the party of seven must be left behind because the canoes could only between them carry six. That, Hiscock explained, would be Godwin's decision which implied that one, some or all of them might as well be resigned to a long and perilous walk to Sweden, a decision he was glad not to have to take himself.

Erling Jøssang came back the next night. He did not mention, nor did the three offer any explanation about, the absence of the four who had departed. He returned the next night too at about the time (though they could not know it) when Godwin was leading the raid on Kopervik, and on each occasion found the Englishmen calm and composed. The third night it was different for them all. For one thing, Jøssang knew about the sinking of the German minesweeper M5207 that morning. There had been three underwater explosions at 0430 hrs, and the ship had rapidly taken on a list and ignominiously rolled onto her beam ends. An hour later there had been a fourth explosion to the conflicting delight and consternation of the Norwegians. The perplexed and annoyed Germans had sent down a diver, but apparently had not the slightest idea of the cause. Jøssang felt pretty sure that the four missing Englishmen were somehow connected with the sinking. Without saying so, Hiscock, Cox and Roe agreed, but with excellent cause.

That afternoon three Germans in a rowing boat had appeared. As usual, whenever fishermen hove into sight, Hiscock and his men had taken cover, preferring Jøssang remained their only contact. This time their precaution had been doubly rewarded. The rowing boat's crew was heading their way. Instinctively, they had asked themselves if they had been seen or had Jøssang betrayed them? Yet surely if their presence was known, a much stronger party would have been sent in a motor boat? So perhaps this was a search party, or an attempt to check out Jøssang's betrayal without disclosure of purpose! Or maybe, of course, they were merely out for an afternoon's pleasure boating! No, the latter seemed most unlikely at a time when the Germans must suspect an enemy presence and be anxious to track it down. Whatever the reason, Hiscock agreed with Cox that if the Germans made one false move they must be killed.

Jack Cox lay behind the Bren grun, hidden from view but with a first-rate field of fire covering the boat should it come close enough to pick out the coble beneath its shroud of seaweed. The two men rowing had their backs to him. The third sat in the stern at the tiller. There was no sign of weapons. The Germans were defenceless—dead ducks when Cox chose. He only hoped his companions would refrain from loosing off prematurely with their popgun stens. This he wanted all to himself with three aimed single shots. No point in wasting ammunition with a half a magazine or so to attract the undivided attention of anybody within earshot. The execution needed to be as unobtrusive as possible to gain the maximim time for escape while the enemy at Klepp deliberated over what the isolated shots had been about—if they even heard them. At last he could make out their close cropped unhelmeted heads and the detail of their leather equipment and arm badges. They rowed as close as that—point blank. The sights were on the head of the man looking in his direction and he was on the point of squeezing the trigger, believing he must be spotted, when the boat turned away. He paused, waiting for a sign from the men's demeanour. But either they were extremely good actors with incredible presence of mind, or they had genuinely failed to see the coble. Two minutes later they were outside the arc of fire, hardly bothering to look back, and soon out of sight beyond the next headland. It was amazing! Unbelievably fortunate! But worrying too.

It was at moments such as that of Jøssang's return that night when the lack of a Norwegian speaker was so serious. Gesticulations and gibberish were no way of precisely transmitting inner feelings and expressions of concern. Although Jøssang thought the British were calm, he realised they were disturbed. A change of location was essential, as they made plain. Justified too was consternation at the signs of a break in the weather as the wind increased from the south-west: certainly, Jøssang was able to convey that this would whip up rough conditions off the west coast of Karmøy. The British had looked hard at each other, appreciating, without disclosure to the Norwegian, that this precluded taking the defective coble to Urter. Sensing a difficulty, Jøssang had suggested that they might prefer to hide on land—on Hognaland, for example—to allow time for the weather to improve. He indicated he would find and make ready a place for the following night. Again they had thanked him profusely and sent him on his way.

Hiscock's decision to leave at once was made easily with the full concurrence of Roe, but with reservations from Cox. The repeated warnings during their briefings and from Godwin about the dangers of becoming too closely involved with Norwegians, however helpful they might be, had to be obeyed. They liked Jøssang and normally would have trusted him absolutely. But who could say what pressures might soon be brought to bear on him and the local populace with threats of reprisal by the Germans for the sinking of their minesweeper? It was essential to put as much distance as possible between themselves and this trap of an enclosed bay before daybreak—commensurate, Cox insisted, with hanging on long enough to meet up with the canoe party. It went right against Cox's training and nature to let his officer down or disobey. Godwin had ordered they must get together again. That was that. But supposing, it was argued, that Jøssang was acting as an agent for the Germans and was trying to keep them in place with the very purpose of allowing the reunion and thus helping the Germans round up all seven commandos in one swoop?

They compromised, agreeing to stay on the island until within an hour of first light, in the confidence that the canoes would have returned by then. Knowing that if the canoes were missing by then, it was likely something fundamental was wrong—which made it all the more important they should find a fresh hide away from the bay.

This spell of waiting was the worst they had experienced to date. As the time dragged by and nobody arrived, growing anxiety for the canoeists slowly overtook them, piling upon concern for the weather and the coble's fitness. Quite as eager as was their desire to be reunited as a group, was the overlying worry about how they might manage without Godwin's resourcefulness — piling on anxiety for their personal safety. Supposing the Germans were already on their way? Could it be they had established an ambush across one of the narrow channels, or were patrol boats already lying in wait? How much had the three men in the boat seen? Who was fooling whom? The time dragged, with Roe the most anxious to beat the gun, Cox pleading for every delay and Hiscock spanning the gap, and as Coxswain making the final decision to go at the time agreed. It was a sad moment when he knew they could wait no longer and with a heavy heart that he gave Roe the order to start up and proceed.

The journey to the mouth of the bay was watchful — cautious for fear of the enemy, alert in the search for a glimpse of the canoes in visibility which closed in as the weather deteriorated. From the start they knew that the chances of seeing the canoes, which for their own preservation would take avoiding action on hearing or seeing another boat, were remote. Inevitably, by the time they had to seek a temporary hide as daylight approached, no contact had been made. With this failure a certain aimlessness seems to have settled upon Hiscock's crew. Despondency at the belief their leader and the young seamen had either been killed or captured was exacerbated by a feeling of the hopelessness of their own situation. Having abandoned any possibility of meeting the MTB on 9 May, they had committed themselves to a lonely venture through unknown waters and country which were hostile in more ways than one. Any indication of enemy activity they put down to the sinking of the minesweeper and a search for themselves.

When they arrived, the following night, on the island of Ogneøy, their spirits were at a low ebb. Despite carefully nursing the revs, the propeller bearings were making such horrible noises that they abandoned the attempt to complete the journey to the mainland. As before, they hid to allow Roe to make repairs, taking the usual precautions of avoiding Norwegians but, eventually, breaking the rules by contacting a farmer to beg for water. From him they heard about German activities — how the hunt had died down a little, but of the imposition on the 8th of a ban upon movement of rowing boats at night on pain of being fired upon. As a result they tarried upon Ogneøy until the night of 11/12, by which time they thought the passage of the narrow straits to the mainland might be safe. For the last time they put to sea in the coble, dumping the bren and sten guns, the ammunition and the remaining limpets, as they made for Susart, but deciding to burn the coble rather than scupper it in shallow waters with every possibility of being found. Hurriedly they had doused her in petrol and planted a delayed-action detonator in the fuel tank before setting off inland with as much food as they could carry, armed with pistols and dressed in their battledress under oilskins.

The going was hard through a tortuous terrain of streams, lakes and forest and farms. Maintaining direction was always a problem, but the snow-capped mountains of the interior beckoned—and Sweden seemed an awfully long way off—in a straight line a good 250 miles and much more than that allowing for impassable country. They dared only to march by night, avoiding the obvious check points and hamlets, sleeping by day in thick cover with shelter from the weather. On 12/13 and 13/14 they totalled only five miles as the crow flies, though much farther taking into account diversions. Here and there they encountered Norwegians. On the first night a bachelor farmer living in solitude found them shelter for the day and pointed them in the direction of Hervik. The second, an old man showed Hiscock a secret pathway through the forest of Hesjadalen. Their's was a haphazard progress made in semi-wilderness by sense of direction without the benefit of an established Norwegian escape organisation to take them in hand.

By then a hue and cry had been raised. Acting as regulations demanded, the Norwegian police had reported early on the 12th the discovery of a completely undamaged open motor boat, which had been found half-beached on a stoney shore at Susart. An attempt to destroy it, they said, had failed. On board were boxes of provisions, a sea chart 'with exact entries of batteries and military installations' and a course plotted as at once to indicate to the Germans a connection with the sinking of M5207. Next day the search for what the Admiral commanding Norwegian coast called 'the landed commando troop' was resumed. Under the direction of Korvetten Kapitan Hermann Jung, the Hako (harbour commandant) Haugesund, army units were put on the track of those who had come ashore at Susart, and a daylight search of possible landing areas and less-frequented bays was begun by the patrol boats as reinforcement of the existing threat to shoot at rowing boats during the hours of darkness.

The soldiers, acting as beaters, employed well-rehearsed methods for scouring the countryside—driving along the most likely escape routes, setting up road blocks, searching isolated buildings and interrogating farmers. They drew a blank in the case of the bachelor farmer, despite threatening him with a pistol. Convincingly he played 'lunatic' until the Germans went away in disgust. With the old man it was different. He was frightened more easily—and venal. One rumour had it that he was bought for a bottle of brandy; another that it cost the Germans 10,000 kroner. Either way, he told the Germans which way the Englishmen had fled and showed them the secret path through the trees.

Without difficulty, a few hours later, a German patrol found Hiscock, Roe and Cox asleep, like the Babes in the Wood, among the trees. So it was that the silent people of Haugesund saw the trio, their heads erect, paraded with pride and in ignominy, through the streets of their town.

13

The Canoe's Story

Except that the wind began to rise and the water turn progressively rougher, the journey from Hallvadsvig to Kjeøyna was uneventful. Moving fast through the sheltered Boknasund while they were fresh, they sighted not a single craft of any kind. Out in the wide Bokna Fjord it was another matter. There they struggled against the stiff breeze and through the uneven surface lop, their speed decreasing the farther south they paddled and the wearier they became. Periodic checks of their position were comforting, however. Even at the reduced pace they were on schedule to enter the enclosed bay with ample time to reach the coble's hide before daybreak.

They approached what they took to be Kjeøyna cautiously. Who knew but what Hiscock's party had been discovered or given away in their absence? In which case the danger of an ambush was possible instead of the welcoming hot meal and drink all four relished. Hesitantly Godwin identified the right inlet, after discussion among the three seamen who agreed that at night one island looked much like another. Guessing that Hiscock's look-out would not necessarily detect their approach or risk a premature challenge, Godwin came ashore a hundred metres off and sent two companions with instructions to confirm the place and make contact.

The advanced guard took its time, putting into practice the scouting techniques taught by Cox, in due course reaching what they now positively recognised, by cloud-diffused moonlight, as the hide and, nearby, the lookout post. Bare of people and coble, of course. Nobody else around either it seemed. So they looked a little closer, just to confirm it was the right place. Yes, here signs of the camp and there, by the water's edge, piled up seaweed which had covered the coble. Also cigarette ends and a discarded packet, indicating a certain carelessness Godwin would not approve of if he was told. But told he had to be as proof they were in the right place and as evidence, possibly, of a hasty departure.

Godwin's reaction was one of anxiety rather than annoyance. It was bad enough that they were deprived of their mobile base with its foodstocks and shelters, particularly now that it was beginning to rain on the wind. From now on, they would have to sleep and survive in the open. Far more worrying were the perplexities of the situation. Why had Hiscock moved? Had he been betrayed and captured or simply given himself away by carelessness? Or had something threatening cropped up? In which case when had he moved, in what direction and how far off was he now? For instance, he might have gone, for local evasion's sake, only a short distance and be in hiding nearby from where he could observe the original hide, placed to remake contact once the canoes had returned. Taking the most optimistic view, which also had the advantage of having more to gain than loose, Godwin opted to act as if the latter was the case. He would at once occupy a hide on a nearby island which he had previously earmarked as an alternative base, and let events develop in daylight. Then, if nothing transpired, he would assume the next most promising eventuality—that Hiscock had felt so endangered as to compel an early start for Urter—perhaps because of an enemy threat, maybe because the coble was so crippled as to be only capable of short hops to safety. In the last resort he had to conclude that either they had abandoned hope and were making for Sweden, or were in enemy hands, or dead. But whatever the location and state of the coble and its crew, Godwin saw no reason to alter the original plan of making for Urter in plenty of time for the pick-up on 9 May—five days hence.

They found a suitable cove among overhanging rocks which gave some shelter on an islet, some 500 yards off, with a good view over the hide on Kjeøyna. From there they kept watch all day and saw only the usual procession of fishing boats, among them Jøssang's, and a patrol boat whose crew seemed to be unusually inquisitive. But neither Jøssang nor anybody else went anywhere near the original hide. Therefore, come nightfall, Godwin, after discussion with the others, felt bound to abandon hope of finding the coble again in that vicinity. With plenty of time in which to reach Urter before the MTB's arrival, Godwin planned to shift by stages of seven to eight miles each night, thus providing a large allowance for delays brought about by foul weather or enemy interference. The only thing he determined to do immediately was to put the Karmsund between himself and Vestre Bokn. In his imagination, the island had begun to assume a sinister meaning due to the coble's unexplained disappearance. So while Hiscock, Roe and Cox in the coble (having missed meeting the canoe by a few hundred yards and a margin of minutes) were setting course for Sweden on the night of 4/5, Godwin, West, Mayor and Burgess were pushing out in the opposite direction across the Karmsund on what was to be a hard slog in the face of wind, swell and choppy water.

The conditions were not, of course, as severe as those Godwin and West had experienced in the Sognefjord in February. But the danger of being over-whelmed by heavy seas or swept out of control onto rocks or to within sight of an enemy post was omnipresent, as also was the possibility of being run down by a passing ship. Keeping in touch was one problem; navigating accurately for an invisible point on the shore of Karmøy, somewhere close to the entrance to Skudeneshavn or Geitungen, another but related. Should they become separated, Godwin had decreed a rendezvous near their intended destination at Alleskjer. On several occasions contact nearly was lost and there were moments when they wondered if they would stay upright and survive. But never did anybody stop paddling or struggling. It was not in their creed to do so. And they were very fit.

Eventually they achieved every goal Godwin had set. They completed the crossing and entered the shelter provided by the islets off Karmøy's southern tip, intact, in company and with time and energy enough to continue their voyage with every hope of reaching the objective before daylight. It was very desirable they should do so. The coastline around Skudeneshavn was quite highly populated with many fishermen. On the other hand, according to the chart, Alleskjer was conveniently desolate; as it proved, although exposed to the buffeting of wind and waves, making a landing adventurous. For that reason, despite the welcome absence of people, Godwin decided to leave the next night, seeking a new refuge which offered a nice compromise between safety, isolation and reasonable proximity to Urter. Yet, even though his resolve to avoid Norwegians remained constant, the need for some kind of help from them was already pressing. Deprived of supplies from the coble (which they keenly imagined finding as of right), they were running short of food and would need to replenish stocks before 9 May.

Next night, the 5/6 May, in easier conditions than the previous night, they continued their journey, reaching the vicinity of Ferkingstad in such good time that Godwin felt justified in making an instant change of plan. Previously he had intended to lurk among small islands to the south of Salvoynaa. Now, in view of the need to replenish the food, it seemed desirable to find somewhere of minimum population where it might be easier to 'live off the land', or from the sea than on Karmøy. Harking back to CRACKERS, there was always a prospect of capturing some unwary sheep and putting to use Burgess's skill as a butcher, with his talent for fleecing a sheep in three minutes. Less than three miles due west of Ferkinstad and eight miles due south of Urter, lay the cluster of Ferkingstadøyane, seemingly ideal to the requirement, and well within striking distance that night. Moreover, it would be unwise not to take advantage of the improved conditions to get closer to Urter just in case the weather again deteriorated before the 9th. If the three seamen had any doubt about heading directly to sea, they kept it to themselves. In any case, they had travelled barely five miles that night and were as keen as Godwin to get as far from the Germans as possible, to a place where they might move around freely in daylight instead of being confined in some cold and damp cell-like hole among rocks.

The islands, they were soon to discover, contained more people than expected, folk who were almost immediately aware of the visitors, quick to guess a connection with the recent sinking at Kopervik and quite unflinching, like the Pedersons and Jøssang, in offering help despite the terrible risks involved. With the tiny island community there was, of course, less risk of disclosure than among the diverse groups on Karmøy or the mainland. Everybody knew everybody else and was interdependent. Nobody had the slightest Quisling leanings — any more than had the Pedersons, Jøssang or all, except that one fatal person whom the coble party had met. So they spent this entire day and the next on Ferkingstadøyane in comfort and without the need to hunt and kill a sheep or any other animal. For as soon as the islanders found that the the Englishmen were short of food and planning to cross the North Sea, they provided fish and tinned food in exchange for such luxuries as coffee, tea and chocolate that their guests still possessed.

Godwin was tempted to remain for a further 24 hours, revelling in the warmth of welcome, knowing that Urter held few if any people and virtually no shelter. But news that the Germans were on the look-out for people who had sunk a boat at Kopervik (the first proof of the success of their attack) prompted him to reassert his initial rule of distancing from the Norwegians. It would be morally unjustifiable to expose such generous people to unnecessary risk, prepared as the islanders were to help in every way they could. So on the night of 7/8 they set forth on the last leg of the journey, paddling by compass due north, realising all too well how easy it might be to miss the low, inconspicuous, unlit islets which were their goal.

There was a feeling of immense exultation when they reached their destination. At last things were going right. There was plenty of time in which to identify the main island in the group and which was easily recognised by the little white painted house standing at one end. This they knew to be a disused building where Kopervik and Haugesund harbour pilots used to wait for ships. Now it housed a single Norwegian fisherman, a seemingly harmless individual but one who posed a threat to security. It was also, Godwin knew, the landmark Knut Bøgeberg on MTB 626 would be seeking on the night of the 9th. Until then the fisherman would have to be kept under close surveillance and prevented from going to the mainland where, even unintentionally, he might divulge their presence. Their one disappointment concerned the coble. Nobody on Ferkingstadøyane had mentioned it. A search of Urter drew blank. Yet time remained for it to turn up if it was in hiding somewhere on Karmøy waiting a last minute opportunity to cross. Meanwhile, as thick mist and driving rain drenched them, they sheltered among clefts in the rocks in discomfort and extreme boredom mitigated entirely by anticipation of proximate rescue from their Crusoe-like state, preferring also to endure the unkind elements and give a wide berth to the comfort of the pilot's house for fear of detection by hostile eyes.

The Spring, which had stirred shortly before their arrival in Norway, had by now broken forth and was greening the dull brown winter's coat of the islands. That alone was cheering. To fill the time they gossiped about old times and what they would do on the first night back in Lerwick, about their families and their girl friends and the joys of leave to follow. Sometimes they sang cheerily, or Godwin would hold quizzes on similar lines to the old training programme back in Scotland. Of greater importance, he also instructed and rehearsed them in a revised cover story just in case—the hourly decreasing case—they were caught by the enemy before that golden midnight hour of the 9th.

'They'll guess we were the blokes who sank that trawler, so there's no need to prolong the agony when questioned. Stick to the fact we belong to Combined Operations but don't mention 14 Commando or anything else like that. Say we expected to be picked up by an MTB but it didn't turn up, so we were going to pinch a fishing boat and take it to Scotland. Don't mention the lot in the coble. They could still be on the run and there's no point starting the Jerries looking for them all over again. And remember we steered clear of Norwegians. So, we had better agree on an imaginary route from Bokn to here so as to make them think we stopped only at uninhabited places. Let's say that little island of Teisthl near Büssolmane, so as to divert attention from the chaps who met us. After that, it's OK to mention any of the hides on the way to and from Kopervik and the one at Alleskjer because nobody saw us there—I suppose. But that last lot of islands we never visited! Tell them, instead, that we spent a couple of days on' [. . . and he studied the chart]'—on, say, those rocky islands close to the south of Salvoynaa at the southwest entrance to Veavaagen, there.'

As part of the time-filling exercise they went over the cover plan again and again until it was committed to memory—even though they never took the gloomy view that they might require it in earnest—not until past midnight on the 9th, that is.

*   *   *   *   *

The weather forecast was unpromising when Knut Bøgeberg took MTB 626 to sea, and it showed no sign of proving false in the approaches to Urter. The typical swell was not what worried him, but the enclosing curtain of mist which made a precise landfall quite impossible and a search for the cluster of islands extremely hazardous. In any conditions these flat bumps rising out of the seaway were a menace to navigation. In mist and darkness they were virtually impossible to locate—and it has to be remembered that 30th Flotillas MTBs were not equipped at that time with radio navigation devices and their radar was to detect aircraft only. Bøgeberg did his best, crawling through the opaque murk with all hands at action stations peering ahead for sight of the slightest mark which might help them fix a position upon which to base an accurate course for Urter—perpetually in fear of running ashore to be left stranded for the enemy once the atmosphere cleared.

A point at which Bøgeberg could persist no longer had to be reached, one where he had to call it off due to total uncertainty of position and the fear that to remain longer would expose them to air attack in daylight. He left it as long as he dared, but in the end had reluctantly to swing west and make for Lerwick.

At the same time the canoe party, convinced at last that the coble was missing irretrievably, had also faced up sadly to the realisation that the mist which cloaked the island could not be penetrated by the MTB. Throughout the night they kept watch, ears cocked for the faintest sound of engines, eyes straining for a dark shape edging in, ready to warn and challenge at once with the special recognition torches. Yet feeling in their bones that a break was impossible, and burrowing into their hides at break of day in a state of acute despondency and dread of the future. At that moment the damp felt colder and wetter than ever it had before, the rocks assuming a prison-like greyness and the meagre food stocks looking quite insufficient for another week.

That day Godwin was hard-pressed to revive his own spirits, let alone those of his depressed companions. Conversation wilted, singing died in the throat, not even a lament seeming appropriate. Towards evening Godwin, who had tried as best he could to revive their cheer, appreciated that morale might collapse completely if nothing was done. At that he decided to risk the consequences and move to the house where they would be warmer and dry. Indeed, he had a feeling that to stay in the open much longer could easily induce a serious physical deterioration with an accumulating drop in morale.

Taking up residence in the hut certainly gave a lift, circumscribed as their occupancy was by Godwin's strict rules that under no circumstances were they to advertise their presence by lights at night, by a fire or by moving around by day in the open. At the same time, he encouraged them by, for the first time, converting an element of the cover plan into a shaft of action, a target to strive for. That is, by giving positive thought to ways and means of seizing a suitable fishing boat if one happened to come close enough to be boarded or if an opportunity arose of paddling to the mainland with a view to cutting one out of harbour. Planning was better than incantations of 'Roll on the 16th'. It kept their minds active and created an alternative course and feeling of hope in case, on the 16th (the next scheduled pick-up date), something went wrong again. They also helped the fisherman to supplement their foodstocks, but he, quite naturally, was becoming more than a trifle concerned about his voluntary incarceration.

With every day that passed, at times with interminable slowness, their hopes began gradually to revive. News of the curfew on rowing boats did not worry them. Failure of patrol craft to investigate the islands closely was an encouragement. On the morning of the 15th, with barely 36 hours left before the MTB was due again, they were feeling hungry but growing excited—and withall a mite careless. For then it was that a patrol boat spotted something which aroused the crew's suspicions. Too much movement around the house by more than one person where a single fisherman only was known to live—and this at the very moment when the hunt for commandos was being intensified upon news that part of a troop had been captured the day before on the mainland.

Towards evening a shout from the watch warned Godwin of something seriously amiss. The man's voice—it was West's—had an unusually urgent note, more of surprise than panic. He ordered 'Stand to' before running to the door to investigate. At once it was clear that West had good cause for concern and perhaps a slight conscience for delay in giving the alarm. Standing in fast were two motor cutters, filled with soldiers, and making to land with drilled deliberation. He cocked his sten gun and heard the others doing the same as they made for the prepared fire positions. All being well, they would take one or two with them, maybe a whole boat load. The first cutter was already within ten yards of the water's edge, the second beginning to swing broadside on, presumably to give supporting fire from what looked like a heavy or medium machine gun. At that moment it occurred to him that it might be rather a quick and bloody affair. He looked across at Burgess and Mayor, tense behind their guns, waiting for the order they expected.

Then he stood up.

14

Rumour and Reality

Despite acute disappointment at the absence of the CHECKMATE party on MTB 626 when she docked at Lerwick, those who had sent them out did not at once fear the worst. It was quite common for men who had been missing for days or weeks—even months or years—to turn up long after they had been officially reported 'Missing'. At this stage the need to send out official letters was unnecessary. No doubt the families would already be worried or surprised that private letters had stopped coming, but people had become accustomed to wartime's irregularities and anxieties and learnt, too, to suppress their curiosity about military affairs. Better no news, the fatalists might argue, than a telegraph boy's knock on the door with the dreaded buff envelope and its bald contents. 'Killed (or wounded) in action. Letters follow.' It was preferable, for a week or two at least, to let those in the know at North Force, ACOS and COHQ take comfort in the circumstances of the failure, and place their trust in Godwin's ability to pull something off, knowing that sooner or later reports from any of a number of sources were likely to provide indications. Above all, confidence that the party, if it had survived, would be waiting on Urter on the 16th.

The first positive evidence that something might have been achieved was noticed on an air photograph taken on 9 May showing a small ship laying on its side in Kopervik harbour. Rumours were more plentiful. From Oslo radio a claim that two men, presumed to be British, had blown themselves up on a landmine in the Bergen area on 4/5 May, and that they had a canoe. Next a report from Intelligence sources concerning the rowing boat curfew on 8 May and, later, a rather vague report via General Hansteen's second in command on a visit to Stockholm, saying SOE had recently blown up a couple of ships in Oslo, along with a rumour of 'a similar job on the west coast'. This Colonel Neville at COHQ felt, 'has a ring of truth about it'.

Hope for the safety of the CHECKMATE party remained quite high, however, when MTB 626 (now commanded by Lieutenant Børresen) sailed to attempt the scheduled 16 May pick-up. This time the visibility was good and landfall made at Urter without difficulty. Warily, Børresen approached the island and gave the recognition signals, but without reply. Always fearful that the Germans might by now be expecting the visit and be lying in ambush, he circled the island before taking the plunge and sending a small party ashore. It was at great risk and a sad blow when absolutely nothing was found to indicate whether or not the men had been there at all.

In a hard war, in which the fate of a few people could so easily be discounted, particularly if others were to be put in peril on their behalf, it says much to the credit of Vice Admiral Wells, to the Norwegian sailors and to Major Ted Fynn that they went on trying to find Godwin and his men. In the space of the next ten days, no less than four separate attempts were made, of which two were foiled on account of fog. On these occasions, commandos were put ashore to either dispose of any lurking Germans and thoroughly to search the island. But to no avail. The final sortie returned on 4 June to signal the end of the enterprise. Next morning a message to that effect lay on Colonel Neville's desk, forcing him to the sad conclusion that the CHECKMATE party was lost and ought, in fairness to the next of kin, to be posted missing. Bureaucracy, in its zealous way, made trebly sure there could be no mistake about it. Between 5 and 11 June, no less than three letters were sent to each family, but with one exception, each containing the same, sparse information that the man concerned had been lost on a hazardous mission; no further details were available. Lieutenant John Shaw of HMS *Fox* it was who offered a ray of hope when he wrote:

> 'This I can tell you, however, and I hope it will bring you some relief in your sorrow. There is an excellent chance of your son's survival, and we are all hoping for better news soon.'

At the same time Neville drafted a letter for Lord Louis Mountbatten to send to Vice Admiral Wells, a document which was to show, in the confusion of war, just how misinformed the authorites were about events. It expressed distress at the loss of 'valuable personnel', and concern that there was 'no indication as to the point at which our plan failed'—indicating that nobody had been made aware of the coble's fundamental weakness. Because the letter went on to state a belief, founded on the Stockholm rumours, that something had been achieved and concluded:

> 'There is no reason why we should not try another of these lying up operations whenever you can spare the craft since it seems the best method by which we can attack shipping on the Norwegian coast at this time of year.'

Hardly had this letter been posted than Neville received yet another relevant message from the Shetlands, this time via the War Office, throwing different light upon the matter. This time the source was reasonably authentic, based upon the report of an Officer Commanding an MTB engaged on a special mission in the North Sea. 'A fisherman', he said, 'had informed him that seven Englishmen were taken prisoner two or three weeks ago at the CHECKMATE rendezvous', a message which prompted Wells to write with relief and gusto to Mountbatten:

> 'It really does look as if they managed to do the task set them and it is certainly good news that they are alive and prisoners. If I know anything of young Godwin we might well hear of him spending Christmas in Stockholm.'

Which amounted to a fair degree of guesswork, in the absence of corroborative evidence, that they had succeeded or if they were all alive. Indeed, there would be an uncertain note struck on 9 July upon receipt of a message from the Intelligence network announcing that 'a reliable source' said:

> 'Three members of the commandos who had been staying for about a week on the small island of Urter were taken prisoner on or about 10 June. The Norwegian who acted as an informer was paid 10,000 kroners by the Germans.'

It probably relieved somebody's feelings at COHQ to scrawl upon the letter '. . . the Quisling will get what is coming to him', but there was still no proof positive that, as another officer minuted, 'This must be the CHECKMATE party', since, of course, the report contained many inaccuracies. It was as well, perhaps, that for the moment no craft or men were available to repeat CHECKMATE, otherwise there was nothing to prevent a recurrence of the tragedy.

*   *   *   *   *

The overriding matter of concern to the German Admiral commanding the Norwegian West Coast was the depredations of MTBs against shipping, with only passing irritation about the damage to a couple of small craft, the net-layer NB06 at Kraakenset-Feuer and the minesweeper M5207 at Kopervik. As for NB06, she apparently had been holed by one of her own mines and was safely beached, while M5207 was more mysterious, although it seemed likely to be a sabotage job, connected with the crew's sighting of a rowing boat a few hours before the explosions, and linked to the mysterious canoe incident at Bergen at about the same time. Incidents such as these were a nuisance, a very serious one if they damaged as many as four large ships as had happened at Bordeaux before Christmas, but in Norway, so far, nothing like as menacing as the battle against MTBs. So while Korvetten Kapitan Jung was told to improve protection of boats lying in harbour and press ahead vigorously for the capture of the men from the landing craft found at Susart, the main effort was directed to the searching of suspicious landing areas and less-frequented bays as part of the MTB war. It was, indeed, as much due to this activity as to the intensification of the search for the rest of the commando party after Hiscock, Roe and Cox were captured at Hervik that suspicion fell on Urter.

PLATE 11.   Charles Herlofson (*binoculars*) controlling an attack from the bridge of his MTB

PLATE 12.   Norwegian visitor to the MTB hide

PLATE 13. Norwegian visitors to the MTB hide

PLATE 14. John Godwin comes aboard an MTB from the coble, while Jack Cox(?) makes fast below

PLATE 15. The canoe element of the CHECKMATE party immediately after capture. Godwin speaks to (*left to right*) Mayor, Burgess and West as he is led away by German officers. Notice the very correct uniform worn by the sailors with the Royal Navy flash clearly visible

15

The Web
of Interrogation

Four men with sten carbines pitted against four times that number armed with machine guns and rifles represent poor odds. By a stroke of luck the four sailors might have taken one or two with them if they had put up resistance, but in truth resistance would have signed Godwin's own death warrant and those of West, Mayor and Burgess. And to him that seemed pointless. As the Germans leapt out of their boats and deployed purposefully into battle formation, Godwin reached the unhappiest decision of his life and ordered his men to throw down their arms, stand up with hands raised in surrender. Later, to the Germans, he was to give as a reason the effect of surprise, but the underlying cause was more profound than that.

> 'Sorry chaps' [he said quickly as the Germans drew close]. 'We nearly made it. But we're not finished yet. Remember what I've told you. Stick to the cover plan. Don't let them bamboozle you into giving anything away. And don't give up. Somehow we'll find a way out.'

In the final minute of freedom he ran his eye over their dress, ensuring they looked like the genuine combatants they actually were, checking they had their caps on to advertise legal status and squash accusations they were mere *franc-tireurs*. In his mind he reviewed the dire meaning of the Commando Order as it had been explained. Under no circumstances must the Germans be allowed to pin that upon them. It was going to be a battle of wits and one he was ill-equipped to fight. But in his heart he knew that to maintain their rights as normal prisoners of war was the only possible way, and he owed it to them all to try to brazen it out. He only hoped that, at last, luck as well as providence would be on their side.

In the act of taking their prisoners, the Germans were thorough yet humane—as was fairly natural bearing in mind that no violence had been offered by either side, no tempers frayed or fears raised as the by-product of resistance; and because the British had surrendered rather supinely, without call. A search of the captives had revealed no hidden weapons. There was a slight rousing of suspicions by the discovery of Norwegian tinned food in the pilot house, but this Godwin managed to explain away, in his rudimentary German language, as having been there when they arrived and probably belonged to the fisherman who, he pointed out, had been an unwilling hostage throughout. The Germans were elated by their coup, the discovery of the two canoes adding to their delight. On the journey to Haugesund, at gun point packed into the cutter, they even began to develop that innate kindred spirit which so often springs up between both sides of genuine fighting men in adverse circumstances.

Those who watched the CHECKMATE party arrive in Haugesund thought they looked downcast but not demoralised. Slightly bedraggled, perhaps, but clean shaven and as tidily dressed as might be expected of disciplined men, wearing camouflaged oilskins over their khaki uniforms and woollen caps at the regulation angle. It was not only obvious to Korvetten Kapitan Jung and Lieutenant Grodler (the lawyer whose duties were those of court or legal officer of Grenadier Regiment 489) that these four were linked to the three brought in from Susart the day before, but that they would need to be interrogated with guile if they were to give better information than the three had as yet divulged. So far those taken at Hervik had told a rather sketchy story—how they had been compelled to abandon their mission and attempt to reach Sweden. Grodler could now see that the coble party had been telling the truth; it genuinely had been unaware of the canoe party's movements since first arrival in Norway. He also could understand why they had split up, since examination of the coble's propeller shaft and the need to tow it to Bergen, instead of going under its own power, had revealed the extent of the damage.

So it may have come as a surprise when the young officer, whom they interrogated first, made but little effort to hide the facts. Face to face with Godwin across the table, Grodler began by trying to throw the Englishman off balance by announcing that he already knew all about the mission from the coble crew, whom they had captured and whose names he read out. The exact impression Godwin made upon his examiners is unrecorded, although they must surely have been gratified, and should have been made suspicious, by the frank and almost submissive manner in which he told them what they wanted to know. To some extent, so swift was Godwin's admission, the inquisition reverted into a straightforward interview. To begin with, Godwin admitted, as was permissible, his name and rank as well as announcing he was in the British Navy and a member of Combined Operations—thus avoiding a breach of security by mention of the secret 14 Commando. The statement he finally signed (and which is reproduced at the end of this chapter) was completed within a few hours, which included the time required to compare it with statements by his companions and for re-examination concerning certain discrepancies. It really does seem likely that Jung and Grodler fell into the same error of misjudgement of Godwin as had several British and Norwegian officers on first acquaintance—thus dropping into the trap set for them.

Cleverly, in response to shrewd lawyer's questioning, Godwin managed to give the broad outline of the story, as per cover plan, but to leave out certain details he felt sure the three sailors would let slip—the tactics employed attacking the minesweeper, the sounding of the alarm by its crew and the arrangement for pick-up by MTB from Urter. Otherwise, it would have sounded word perfect immediately. As he expected, they would, after putting West, Mayor and Burgess through a much shorter examination, return to him, inexorably worming out the missing information, grimly persuading him to explain that he did not know how the limpets worked, only how to operate them, and hearing him throw in, for good measure, the information that the canoes were only propelled by paddles. Finally having to admit, in a correction to this first statement, that weather permitting, an English torpedo boat was to have picked them up at Urter, but this had fallen through, yet without providing the slightest hint that a subsequent attempt was planned.

The statement shows how completely the Germans were fooled by just large enough a margin to allay any suspicion falling upon Norwegians or to place MTBs in hazard when next they visited Urter. And the fact that this statement alone was kept on the German record indicates that there was scarcely any divergence by the other six members of the party. Indeed, although somebody did manage to obtain from Mayor an admission that they had exchanged chocolate, tobacco and coffee with some Norwegians, there is only one known instance of a Norwegian being arrested for involvement, and he, unfortunate fellow, was the man at Ogneøy who gave water to Hiscock, Roe and Cox.

The question arises, how hard did the two Germans strive to obtain a full confession and, asked in the full context of the situation, why were they so easily beguiled? Were they genuinely satisfied with the answers they received or were they worried about what might happen next to their prisoners, bearing in mind that they were perfectly aware of the Hitler Commando Order and can have had little doubt about the fate reserved for anybody suspected of being a saboteur or commando? For Standing Orders laid down that commandos had to be handed over to the SD (SS Security Service) for counter-intelligence questioning, which, as most officers knew, implied imprisonment under severe conditions or execution. The length of time between interrogation by the armed forces and handing over to the SD might vary, but in Norway it tended to be short. Of course there were occasions when the rules were broken, notoriously so in the immediate aftermath of the promulgation of the Commando Order, during which several commando soldiers in Norway, and elsewhere, had been shot. But gradually revulsion, plus an inbuilt morality, began to make itself felt within the armed forces. To a majority the Order was objectionable, but being bound by regulations (and few people can be so meticulous in obedience to the letter of the law as the Germans) members of the armed forces attempted sometimes to circumvent the Order by placing captured commandos in a safe category before washing their hands of the matter when handing them over to the SD. And safe categories there were, contained within caveats to the Order which stated that:

> 'This order does not apply to the treatment of any soldiers who, in the course of normal hostilities . . . are captured in battle or give themselves up. Nor does this order apply to enemy soldiers falling into our hands after battles at sea. . . .'

Arguably the CHECKMATE party fell within this category. So it was with mild relief that Jung and Grodler, having established through Godwin's confession and their own reports that these were sailors and soldiers captured in battle after a legitimate attack upon a naval target, passed the papers to their Admiral who as rapidly, on 16 May, 'as instructed', handed them over to the SD.

An uninformed or insensitive person might accuse John Godwin of taking the easy way out and interpret his surrender to coercion as an act of weakness, if not of cowardice. Nothing about Godwin's record during manhood supports this standpoint. Most of the evidence, in fact, points in the opposite direction, towards the habit of clinging to his purpose all the more resolutely when confronted by oppression. How much Godwin examined himself in this connection is, however, quite another and undisclosed matter. Being of good conscience, he was bound to reassess his performance in an attempt to satisfy himself and recognise his mistakes. Ducking an issue was not among his characteristics. Having balanced the awesome strength of the enemy against an apparent gullibility he had previously encountered among Germans of his acquaintance in Argentina, he recognised that it was possible to dupe his captors and, with any luck, save all their lives. Although 24 hours later he would have cause to revise that assessment.

Awaiting them in Stavanger were the minions of Heinrich Himmler whose SS (Schutz Staffeln) formed Adolf Hitler's praetorian guard, staffed the SD, the Gestapo, the special extermination units and the concentration camps, and whose ramifications of a state within the State spread wide to include private industrial concerns and their own arm of the fighting services, the Waffen SS. Confident in the craft of terrorism which they had imposed upon the Third Reich, they discounted the possibility of prolonged resistance to their wiles by an insignificant band of commandos upon whom they confidently expected quickly to pin irrefutable charges of sabotage. Their victims were despatched by the first available vessel from Haugesund passing to starboard Kopervik quay where salvage operations on the sunken minesweeper were on the verge of completion and providing Godwin with a reflective moment of uplift as he communed with his men for the first time since their capture.

They had to avoid indiscretions for fear they were overheard, a caution they had begun gradually to acquire from the start of their imprisonment as the implications of several questions sank home. In the short time at his disposal, Godwin's aim was to compare notes between the coble and canoe party and congratulate Hiscock and his group upon coming through alive, adding how sorry he was they had been foiled in the escape bid. Recriminations were avoided, as also was a post mortem on such controversial subjects as the defects of the original plan and the failure to reunite after the attack on Kopervik. Only the future mattered. They had to concentrate undividedly now upon defeating quite another type of enemy to the one they had initially set out to conquer. Everything had to be thrown into the battle to overcome shock and rebuild morale and resolution by creating among themselves a united front founded upon understanding and dominant leadership by example. Maybe it did not appear as crystal clear as that to begin with to Godwin. And he, as well, was dependent for help and encouragement from the phlegmatic Hiscock, the ever cheerful and dauntless Cox, the slightly stunned Roe and the inherently optimistic West, Mayor and Burgess, to whom, in youthful optimism, the full scale of their predicament was yet to be understood. Trying to measure up to the unimaginable in a mere hour asked a lot of intelligence and insight.

Stavanger gaol with its sombre cells provided a fitting introduction to the next grim phase of their ordeal. British raiders had been held there before, bullied by SD and Gestapo. Prominent among them, towards the end of 1942, were the five Royal Engineers who had survived a crash in their glider while engaged in Operation FRESHMAN *en route* to blow up the Rjukan electricity plant with its facility to make the heavy water needed for research into atomic power. They had been packed into one small, cold cell, their injuries only partially attended to, awaiting the predetermined day of execution by shooting. As the CHECKMATE party were at once to discover, the SD started an investigation on the assumption that the subject was guilty and spent its time manufacturing evidence to fit that hypothesis. Whereas the trusting gentlemen of the armed forces at Haugesund had been content to believe they were dealing with genuine British fighting men, the obsessively suspicious creatures at Stavanger were ruthlessly determined to trick their victims into a confession, true or false, to satisfy vengeful superior officers who judged results by executions.

More than ten years' of trial and error had developed SD techniques to a peak of sophistication and depravity. Local variations there were, depending upon the whim and experience of the expert in charge. At Stavanger at this time they tended, contrary to the Geneva conventions as applied to prisoners of war, to favour degradation, justifying this process on the grounds that commandos and saboteurs were ineligible for prisoner of war status and, as a matter of course, neglecting to report their presence to the Red Cross authorities.

Alternately herded into a single squalid cell or taken out for questioning and hectoring in isolation, the CHECKMATE party found itself becoming mentally undermined as their fitness began to decline from shortage of sleep and a miserably poor diet of thin soup and the black bread to which they were as yet unaccustomed. To some extent their previous outstanding health acted as a bulwark to this treatment, but lack of fresh air and exercise (to which they were restricted to between only five or ten minutes each night) worked its ravaging effect. This was torture of the most refined modern kind, designed to break a man without resort to physical violence; for to have done that might have infringed one of the self-imposed rules of the Nazi racial code, being a violation of the bodies of favoured Nordic peoples. To select Scandinavians, the British and, of course, the Germans, proper cultured respect was due. Of course deprivation, threats and bullying in the traditional barrack square manner were in order as part of the summary powers granted to SS underlings. But formal punishment of the severest kind had to have the stamp of legality upon it which, in the case of Godwin's crew, was unattainable until a lot more proof was unearthed.

From the start the SD had several distinct advantages. Their uniforms were immaculate upon sturdy physiques, their hair neatly cropped and their intelligent and domineering composure gave them an air of invincibility. Not only did they look tough and hold all the trumps, they were confronted by dishevelled wretches who were hungry, weary, beginning to smell a little, who were very frightened and at a loss to know what form the game would take. And yet, for their task, the SD was at one fundamental and as yet unrecognised disadvantage because they based their inquisition upon previous experience of raiders sent to Norway, without apprehending that the CHECKMATE party was unique and not of the underground SOE sort with Norwegian personnel and contacts. Given a few leads, and usually it had been easy enough to demolish the cover story of operatives who were living a lie and under terrible pressure from skilled questioning. When confronted by men who stuck to a fundamentally true story and who were genuinely puzzled when subtle propositions were put to them, and the system was thrown out of gear. We do not know how long it took the Germans to admit they were baffled by confrontation with an incontestibly properly constituted military group, engaged upon a legitimate operation of war, taken in arms and properly attired in a recognised British uniform. Unlike the FRESHMAN party, whose men had worn black underclothing which was rated as a penal irregularity, Godwin's men were correct in every detail of dress. At this point it would have been easy enough to save time and either liquidate Godwin and his men out of hand or transfer them back to the armed services as ordinary prisoners of war.

The CHECKMATE party had become of the highest importance in principle to the SS, not only as a challenge to the professional reputation of the SD as interrogators, but to the Gestapo who wished to create a cast iron precedent for the future condemnation of saboteurs in Norway. It was said that *Brigadeführer* Fehlis, head of the Gestapo in Norway, took a personal interest in the questioning, in which case he would have been under pressure from Reich Commissioner Terboven in Oslo and, possibly, Himmler himself at the centre of the SS web in Oranienburg in Germany. Like all revolutionaries and extremist organisations, the SS was sensitive to being made to look silly before the rivals it was endeavouring to supplant—and the armed forces, who disliked and feared the SS, were always delighted to witness SS discomforture. So, as a change of tack to trick the irritating British sailors, the SD set out to prove to its own satisfaction that the prisoners, after all, actually were Norwegians and not British. Adopting tactics similar to those employed against the FRESHMAN party, they brought in a Norwegian interpreter to see if he could recognise Norwegian intonations. Variations in the dialect of their prisoners may have caused this approach. There were considerable differences between the officer's well-modulated speech, Hiscock's Newfoundland drawl, Roe's mild Cockney, Cox's Somerset burr, the Glaswegian Scottish of West, the ripe Lancashire of Mayor and the broad Yorkshire of Burgess. No doubt the Germans were puzzled, to some extent confused, wondering if, perhaps, they were being hoaxed. It is hard to believe they would have proceeded the way they did for any other reason.

On and on the questions would roll, beginning on a note of calm assurance which sought to disarm and then entrap:

> 'Please do not bother to deny it. We know perfectly well from a number of people on Karmøy and elsewhere that you are Norwegians. They have told us, you see. It will save a lot of trouble if you will now admit it and then we will see what can be done.'

Then later, in a tone of slight exasperation, after 'common sense' had failed to appear, the logical touch:

> 'Why should you be any different to those who have come here before? You know perfectly well, as we do, that all sabotage groups like yours are made up entirely of Norwegians or have a number of Norwegians with them. Tell me why you should be unique? We would be interested. We are not fools, you know!'

Next derision:

> 'Don't be ridiculous. If you are not Norwegians, how did you manage to speak to all those Norwegians on Karmøy and Bokn? We know you did because they have told us. I will tell you, we find it difficult enough to talk to these people ourselves and our language is alike to their's. So how can you have managed unless you are one of them?'

And so on and on until patience began to fray and the interrogator's voice began to rise in anger and frustration when the replies revealed nothing of substance. For at times the Germans began to sense an underlying dumb insolence in their victims, little realising how close Godwin always was to teasing his tormentors by pretending to agree with their inept assertions. Until, that is, he recalled MI 9's warning of only a few weeks ago when it had indicated the danger to Norwegians caught in uniform and how this might be construed as treachery to the German-recognised Quisling government which was denied uniformed forces of its own. Admit to that, even with wry humour, and they might as well fire the fatal shots themselves, with only the Germans any better off.

Against less ill-briefed and, above all, poorly commanded men, the German ruse might easily have succeeded. As it was, the attraction to settle for the seemingly innocuous change in nationality was seductive when urged by the 'soft sell' interrogator, the officer who appeared, after an abortive session of threats and bluster had come to nought, to offer cigarettes, sympathy and balm. Now he was pleading with them:

> 'For God's sake seize this golden opportunity. I know these people and I cannot agree with everything they do. I am a schoolmaster in peacetime, you know. They're convinced you're commandos and you know what that means! Give them what they want. Say you're Norwegians and leave the rest to me. I will have you registered and shunted off to one of the Norwegian prison camps, with any luck to Grini near Oslo, and there you'll be safe. They'll not be able to touch you for we Germans, whatever you may think of us, we do abide by the law.'

They would have taken the bait had not Godwin remembered the MI 9 warning and managed to convince his comrades of its portent, adding that even if he was wrong, the result could hardly be worse than that threatened. So the CHECKMATE party held out until the day the SD had to admit failure. It was, of course, to SS minds only a temporary setback, but more pressing matters were beginning to place fresh demands upon their time. With the arrival of summer and the very long nights of June, the prospects of an Allied invasion of Norway again assumed prominence in the intuitive mind of Adolf Hitler—a fantasy corroborated, in some measure, by the rising tide of Norwegian intransigence, the swelling anger of a people who were increasingly tired of being pushed around and to whom the news of repeated Allied victories from every front acted as a stimulant to 'rowing'.

For the time being, therefore, until fresh evidence could be gleaned or some slip of the tongue added weight to admittedly unproven charges, the British would be kept in SS custody, in the limbo of suspense in order to prevent the armed services asserting rights of possession and transfer to conventional prisoner-of-war camps. By a neat metamorphosis, which went part way to satisfy the SD conviction of a Norwegian relationship, came the arbitrary pronouncement that they *were* Norwegians, would be treated as such and given Norwegian identity and sent to a Norwegian prison where, under SS supervision and amplified harassment, they would be given a Norwegian prison number and expunged from the records as recognised Allied nationals with rights under the Geneva conventions.

GODWIN'S INTERROGATION

Port Commandant Haugesund   Haugesund, 15.5.1945

SECRET

Re the person:
My name is John Godwin. I am a sub-lieutenant in the British Navy. I was born on the 13.12.1919 in Buenos Aires of British nationality and I am a member of the Combined Operations.
Concering the matter
I had the order to attack merchant ships in Kopervik with magnetic mines. For this purpose I was despatched with 6 men of my formation. In a 'Landing Craft Personnel' we were towed to the Norwegian coast by a motor torpedo boat, in fact to a point approx. 4 sm to the west of the south point Karmøy. We arrived there on the 29.4 at 22.00 hrs. We then proceeded under our own steam. Under the south point of Karmøy, the boat developed engine failure (*sic*) so that we did not reach the south point of the island Bokn until the 30.4 at 0700 hrs. We found ourselves under the battery Bokn, where the crew were just cleaning the guns. We were not noticed. We remained in the same place all day. During the night the landing craft was hidden amongst the cliffs and 3 men remained. I myself and 3 men proceeded in two small collapsible boats east of the island Bokn to the north and turned around the north point of the island into Karmsund. We then went along the Karmsund up north as far as Dua, north-east of Kopervik on the island Fosenøy, where we remained on the beach all day on the look-out for ships. But there were no ships anchored in Kopervik which made an attack worthwhile, equally not a single ship sailed through the Karmsund. We remained on the north point of Bokn (Boknehove) for the whole of 1 May and stayed at Dua for the whole of 2 May. In Kopervik I saw only one small minesweeper anchored on the steamship quay. As no other ship came, I decided to attack it during the night of the 2.5 to the 3.5. At 0030 hrs. on the 3.5 we proceeded with our small collapsible boats alongside the minesweeper and attached 4 magnetic mines. The distance from the ship's side was approx. 6 feet. We then moved out of the harbour unnoticed, using small

paddles. As until now I had lost a lot of time, as I had only to wait and no ships came, I decided to immediately make our way back. I still had 4 magnetic mines. I threw these overboard. From 3 May until the night of the 4.5 I was back again on the coast at the north point of Bokn near Hallvarde Vik. During the night of the 3rd to the 4th I went further east of Bokn island to the south and stayed over the 4th on the south point of Bokn island near Teisthl. I could no longer find my landing craft which I had left behind. I now decided—the torpedo motor boat which was promised to pick me up did not arrive—to make my way with my collapsible boats to the island group Urter in order to obtain, in one way or another, a seaworthy Norwegian cutter with which I could sail back to England. I knew Urter to be an isolated, only thinly populated, group of islands. During the night of the 4th to the 5th, I stayed hidden on the west coast of Kermøy and reached Alleskj on the southwest coast of Kamøy on the morning of the 5th. During the night of the 5th to the 6th, I arrived at the rocky islands to the south of Salvoynaa at the south-west entrance to Veavaagen. We reached Urter during the night of the 6th to the 7th. We stayed in Urter until today. We waited for an opportunity to be able to seize a seaworthy Norwegian cutter. We saw no chance to proceed with our collapsible boats, considering the bad weather, the stormy sea and rain. We did not see a suitable cutter either. We stayed for 4 days amongst the cliffs in the shelter of large rocks, to protect us from the rain to a certain extent. Then we moved into an empty house, in which we found Norwegian canned food. Apart from us, only one Norwegian fisherman lived on the island. Today on the 15.5, towards evening my watch reported to me that 2 motor cutters were approaching the island. From one cutter 8 German marines landed and approached us. We put up our hands and were taken prisoner, we were completely taken by surprise.

I was not informed regarding the type and construction of the magnetic mines, we were merely instructed how to handle them. During the whole operation I wore my present suit. With regard to the attack on the minesweeper in Kopervik, I must add: I travelled with my collapsible boat alone alongside the ship's side and attached all 4 mines without being noticed in the shadow of the ship's side. My second collapsible boat was further away to observe. I had completed my task and was already in the process of departing when my second boat came near the attacked minesweeper. Suddenly, soldiers on the minesweeper could be heard running about and a shout: 'Attention a boat.' However, nothing happened and my second boat too departed again without being noticed. I mention in addition that we propelled the two collapsible boats with paddles only, we had no other propulsive power.

With regard to my intention to return to England via Urter, I correct my previous statement: In England I had received orders, as a last resort, to seek out the Urter island group for the return. From there I was promised, weather permitting, to be picked up again by an English torpedo boat.

The record was correctly translated to the prisoner in the presence of the undersigned witness. The prisoner thereupon acknowledged the statement to be reproduced correctly and truly.

Signed JOHN GODWIN

Completed:
signed Hermann A. K. Jung
Lieutenant Commander and
Harbour Commandant Haugesund

As witness:
signed Grodler
Lieutenant and Court Legal Officer
Grenadier Reg. 489

16

Grini Interlude

The mere stroke of a pen in some SS lawyer's office could not, of course, eliminate from Allied force's knowledge of the CHECKMATE party's survival. Strong as Stavanger gaol might look against escape (and right from the beginning Godwin and his companions had it in mind that as a group their duty was to escape), it was far from proof against leakage of information about what went on within. For example, the Norwegian interpreter who had been called in to speak to the FRESHMAN party had transmitted a report via Norwegian agents to London which explained why the Royal Engineers had been shot. It was on the basis of his report that such care was taken from the start to have Godwin and his men wear correct uniforms, also to avoid providing them with kroner or false Norwegian documents. Possession of these had been used as evidence against the FRESHMAN group and led to their deaths. Within a few days London had positive evidence of the whereabouts of the CHECKMATE party in Stavanger gaol, intelligence which was passed to North Force and inspired Fynn and Waggett to make an unofficial study of ways and means of 'springing' their comrades at the first opportunity.

Time was short and information insufficient about the gaol's layout, its defences and the whereabouts of each prisoner. Fynn, Waggett and No. 12 Commando were already earmarked for raiding elsewhere across the English Channel. Intelligence about the outer defences of Stavanger was profuse, and this acted as a deterrent, for those defences were formidable and constantly being strengthened. Moreover, if they could be penetrated, there was barely a chance of reaching the gaol unless complete surprise was achieved. So it promised to be extremely hit and miss, finding the prisoners within the gaol and then escaping. It amounted to a noble thought by loyal comrades whose sense of military realism rapidly convinced them of the project's impossibility. In any case, rejection was fortunate because the CHECKMATE party would have departed before the attempt was made.

On or about 10 June, Godwin and his companions were taken from the gaol and put on a railway train bound, it was said, for Oslo. Automatically their hopes were lifted. At least this journey was unlikely to be to a place of execution, as they had always fearfully expected. Furthermore, since the questioning had stopped, they had been allowed to clean up and the food seemed slightly to improve. It was so wonderful to breath fresh air in the full light of a June day and get on the move, relieved of the boredom of imprisonment. From the depths of despair, they were, of course, extremely prone to grasp at the thinnest of straws. But weakened as their physical state was, there could be no denying a distinct change. For one thing, they were no longer alone. Blinking in the sunlight they had for so long been without, they could see travelling companions—Norwegians also being marched to the lorries which were to take them to the railway station.

The presence in the gaol of the British, whom rumour described as airmen, was known to many of the Norwegians whose curiosity was matched only by their desire to make contact and lend help if they could. During the journey, winding through dales, past the mountains of Agder and Telemark, rearing up to the left, and the coastal waters fleetingly visible to the right, the CHECKMATE party was, for the first time since entering captivity, permitted sufficient freedom to enable conversation with Norwegians. Long before the train had shuffled its way to within sight of the Oslo Fjord and the outskirts of the city, the friendly intercourse which would ensure their future had en-wrapped the British. Entirely unsolicited, the Norwegians began to share what little they had with men who were prepared to fight on Norway's behalf. The gift of cigarettes was merely the first token of a gratitude and, later, an admiration which was to prove boundless and an inspiration.

By common consent, the exchange of information during that journey was restrained. Along with the British, there were Norwegians with secrets they dared not mention and who were perpetually worried lest one among them was a 'planted' eavesdropper working for the SD. Rumours of treachery abounded. It was said that the hard core Quislings, torn by anxiety for the faltering German cause and with their own position threatened, were more willing than ever to supply information to their masters. It was common knowledge, in the aftermath of the recent breakdown of Quisling's political initiative, that the largest ever round-up of dissident or potentially dissident people had begun, a figure of 90,000 people earmarked for transportation to Germany being rumoured. Godwin's travelling companions were of this number, part of a batch of over a thousand military officers, nearly 300 'unreliable' policemen and several hundred university students who were to be denied active 'rowing' at a time when more and more people were convinced Germany had lost the war. The fate of those gathered in was uncertain. Many would find their way into prisons in Norway where visits from relatives were allowed and from whence limited parole was occasionally arranged. A considerable number would be sent to camps in Germany, ostensibly for labour, principally to reduce the risk of insurrection in Norway. A few score had already been executed in Norway for active resistance and sabotage. Many more had disappeared and would never be heard of again.

They came to Grini, close by Roa, some 25 miles north of Oslo and saw, silhouetted against the dark wooded hills, the garish, three-storied red brick prison block dominating many rows of newly built huts, with pitched roofs, fenced in by high wire and guarded at corners and sides by tall watch towers. They noticed the prisoners lined up on the *appelplatz*, enduring another of the regular and sometimes interminable counting sessions, and registered the ill-fitting, baggy uniforms worn which had once done duty as fatigue dress for the Royal Guards. And they heard coarse, guttural SS camp guards shouting with repetitive and limited invective 'Los, Los, Mensch! Verdammte Arschlooch! Schweinerien, Schweinhund', along with similar pleasantries, and a stream of army barrack square commands. This was Godwin's next battleground. Having survived ordeal by the SD, and thus deflected the SS's dagger, he had now to be tested by Himmler's bludgeon, the muscled bullies of the concentration camp service.

At once the CHECKMATE party was selected for special treatment. No sooner had they been documented and allocated numbers, as if they were Norwegians, than they were marched to the central block and incarcerated in what was known as the *Einselhaft* (solitary confinement area) on the second floor of the north wing. Here No. 8007 Godwin was put in a cell on his own, while 8005 Burgess, 8006 Cox, 8008 Hiscock, 8009 Mayor, 8010 Roe and 8011 West were paired. The bunks had boards missing; there were neither mattresses nor blankets. Clearly their trial was to continue.

Yet conditions were far better than at Stavanger, indicating that, at least, the immediate threat of execution had passed. The food was vastly superior and more of it. For breakfast, three slices of heavy bread, a pat of butter and watery, unsweetened coffee of indeterminate pedigree. For lunch, an unappetizing soup as it was named—with lonely pieces of meat or fish floating among the potatoes. And for supper, breakfast over again with the addition, occasionally, of a small cube of cheese or a dab of stewed apple.

> 'Enough?' [asked Odd Nansen (son of Norway's greatest man Fridtjof Nansen) in his *Day after Day*, a record of life at Grini]. 'No, not precisely enough, but I can always get along, my work is not hard. It is worse for the young fellows . . . on heavy work. They get too little. Therefore one must make a point of helping them to some more.'

Immobilised in their cramped cells, the CHECKMATE party could also get along, might even have been able to recuperate their strength if only they could have taken more exercise in the fresh air than the permitted ten-minute airing after dark. At once the sharing of extra food, brought in privately to the camp, was extended to the British through the well-developed communication and supply channels between cells in the *Einselhaft*. For those being punished by a spell of 'bread and water', food could be transferred at night from one top window to the next in a sock suspended on a long pole. But it was the communication system which immediately embraced Godwin and his companions. Knocks on cell walls attracted their attention to the air holes through which messages could be relayed not only the length of the wing but carried also to and from the outside world by the 'string mail'—a line connecting, externally at night by rope and basket, with the *Revier* (hospital) on the third floor above.

Easily overcoming language difficulties while establishing the identity and reason for the presence of the seven Englishmen, the Norwegians offered, along with writing materials, to send letters from each man to England. In less than four days those letters reporting their adventures and the nature of their treatment had been written and lifted to the *Revier*, with a special message from Godwin to all the Norwegians in the camp, an epistle which illustrated his flamboyant style of exhortation as he strove to lift both his own men and his country's allies.

'Hallo Norway.

In the name of King Haakon and King George, greetings and good luck. Last night we received your letter and the letter from our two friends for which many thanks are due for their safe delivery. We had only time to scratch you a few lines last night. So we are sending you this reply. In England we were always told about the wonderful fight that was continued in Norway by your patriots and the thousands like you who had been lucky enough not to have found their way here. But it is with a feeling of great pride that we can sit down and write congratulations to Norway and indeed the civilised world's defenders. A few privileged persons such as we seven Englishmen have had the opportunity to see with our own eyes the work that is being carried out by your countrymen. Before our capture, we were gadding about in Norway for 15 days, and to tell of the help we received from your fishermen at great personal risk to themselves would fill a book. Your soldiers and sailors in England are fine examples of your race and we have many good friends amongst them. And with the training they have received in Great Britain they should give an excellent account of themselves in the liberation of this country.'

The risks involved in message-passing by these means were all too obvious. One trembles at the outcome if Godwin's letters to the Norwegians or to England had been intercepted instead of remaining a guarded, secret inspiration, preserved for post-war reproduction in Norway as part of the Godwin saga. Outgoing messages travelled in all manner of receptacles from cigarettes and matchboxes to lengths of piping on their way for repair, or rolled in the hollow legs of fish boxes being returned empty to Oslo market because they were claimed by the dealers as in short supply. From thence, transmission would be the responsibility of the secret army organisation Milorg, by courier to Norwegian and British agencies in Stockholm or, for urgent matters, by secret radio.

Preparation of messages often took place in the *Revier*. Here Godwin's report and the letters had been wrapped in a toilet paper packet, boldly labelled 'English Legation Stockholm', and placed beneath Nansen's sketch book on the table when the Camp Commandant and Camp Adjutant, clean contrary to the normal routine, burst in. The habitually inebriated *Obersturmbannführer* Seidler—the Storm Drunk, as Nansen calls him—was ever suspicious of Nansen for his influence and his friendship with the Royal Family. This time he was bent on examining Nansen's books to find out if they were 'suitable'— meaning not written by a Jew. Pale with terror, Nansen and his friends attempted to distract the Commandant's attention by picking up all the books they could and piling them upon the table. But before they were able to cover the sketch book, the adjutant had seized it, waved it about in the air and slammed it back on the table—without, by some miracle, revealing or dislodging the incriminating packet.

It requires little imagination to visualise the repercussions of the Germans finding those deadly messages. Not only would Nansen and many more in Grini have been court martialled and, very likely, executed, so too might several fishermen and innocent folk around Karmøy have met their doom, while Godwin and his six companions would at last have been made defenceless. As it was, an apparently corrupted précis of the report (but not, it seems, the letters, since they were never delivered to the next of kin) did reach the British naval attaché in Stockholm who, on 7 July, transmitted to London the news that 'Lieutenant John Gowen RN (*sic*) and six men were in Grini after being captured at Haugesund' and 'Their subsequent transfer to a POW camp was expected.'

The forecast of transfer to a POW camp was highly speculative and could hardly have been permitted by anybody aware of the contest between the Camp Commandant and Godwin. Seidler, as his rank and behaviour advertised, was one of the old-guard Nazi Party strong-arm squad, recruited from the *Sturm Abteilung* into the so-called élite SS and there promoted beyond his capabilities. When drunk, as more often than not he was, Seidler, with sadistic smirk, half-closed eyes, yellowed teeth and flabby grin would reel about the parade ground and through the prison buildings, ferreting out minor faults, checking prisoners for misdemeanours (such as poor saluting or unbuttoned tunics) and creating the chaos which set the example followed by the majority of his officers, his lady secretary and his obedient underlings. Instances of commandant and cronies rampaging through the camp, drunk as lords (and ladies, presumably), screeching and hooting, occurred in parallel with streams of illogical and impractical commands shouted at guards and prisoners alike, who frequently concurred, knowing it would be wiser to delay obedience in the likelihood that the orders would soon be forgotten or superseded. Yet, although there were SS who confidentially admitted to their Norwegian charges that scenes such as these made them ashamed to be Germans, they saw but little hope of salvation. One of them might tell Nansen, for example, that the German people had become too thoroughly subdued under the whip to venture on any counter-action. Another might imply that because 'we have left off thinking' that was 'the right thing'.

> 'Fancy if everyone had his opinion—it would never do. It used to be like that in Germany—that was, the ruin of us. The squabbling. People would never agree. Our Leader has brought us to agree—united us.'

That was the propaganda line Seidler would try to teach Godwin whenever they had their conversations. As Seidler let it be known, 'the important prisoners' demanded special attention. Mainly through an interpreter, he interviewed them, though concentrating on Godwin. Depending upon his temper and the amount of alcohol he had consumed, these 'chats' quite often pursued political themes, as Seidler endeavoured to explain the ineptitude of the English and the benefits to Europe of a unified system under German hegemony. In reply, Godwin, sensing the 'mood of the day', would sometimes do what he had only contemplated at Stavanger—lead the German on—pull his leg by agreeing that 'the German way of life was good, a real example in a good Europe'. Then, for the amused benefit of Norwegians and British within earshot, shouting at the top of his voice: 'There are no slaves in German Europe.' Episodes such as these, reported through 'string mail' and via the Norwegian internal network, which was as eager to pass on heartening news as it was matters of grave substance, won for the CHECKMATE party a reputation for courage and good humour which evoked the highest admiration and ensured they would never, not even more than forty years later, be forgotten.

It was extremely comforting and encouraging for Godwin and the others to feel the Norwegian internees behind them and know they had many, mostly unseen, friends to call upon. Yet escape, the subject they would most like to have discussed and developed, was firmly rejected. Had there been any escapes from Grini, they might ask? Answer: none so far. Why not? There is one overriding reason. From the start the Germans have threatened to shoot 10 to 12 prisoners for every man who escapes, and although they have only once been put to the test and did not carry out the threat, we think they might do so now. We all dream of escape and plot it, but also we must have regard for the others and hold back. This was disappointing to the CHECKMATE party who were so accustomed by training to physical activity and to whom pacifism was almost intolerable. The boredom of being penned within a sweatbox cell with virtually no room in which to exercise, and from which nothing of the outside world could be seen, sapped their morale, straining their will to resist the misery of a medieval-like imprisonment. Yet no doubt it was the Norwegian moral support which kept them in hope and sanity.

The climate of torment waxed and waned in accordance with the Storm Drunk's alcoholic intake, the weather and Germany's declining fortunes at war. Hot July days which, to the distress of inmates, raised each cell's temperature, also raised Seidler's thirst and made him the more unpredictably sadistic and violent. Reports on radio and in the newspapers of the pounding of German cities by Allied bombers preyed heavily upon German guards, who constantly worried for the safety of families and property at home, and who supplemented the official communiqués by, contrary to regulations, listening to the Swedish radio and to the British Broadcasting Corporation — as also did the prisoners on a hidden receiver. News of a much trumpeted offensive against the Russian salient at Kursk on 5 July, with claims of smashing losses inflicted on the enemy, was almost at once offset by a staggering blow. An Anglo-American Army had landed from the sea in Sicily and was sweeping across the island to establish the first firm foothold in southern Europe since 1941. At once it was noted that even members of the camp staff were showing signs of 'rowing', a reaction which was countered on 12 July by the sudden descent upon the camp of some 70 SS men on motor cycles who proceeded to ransack the huts and cells for illicit objects, such as tools and radios, plus the thousands of kroner stored away in air vents and beneath furniture and floorboards against the day of the next transport of prisoners to Germany. This was merely a prelude to larger scale persecution as one disaster after another piled in upon the Germans.

Each admission of a set-back — the vast Russian counter-offensive, hurling back the defeated army in Russia, the retreat in Sicily, the deposition of Mussolini in Italy and the incineration by bombers of Hamburg — provoked vengeance by the camp staff. When the prisoners rejoiced in a whirl of glee at news of Mussolini's sacking and framed the new command 'Musse ab', the SS retaliated by submitting some inmates to an evening's punishment drill of which, as Nansen wrote:

> 'All SD officers except the Camp Commandant (who was too lazy no doubt) took part in the punishing, which became an absolute orgy. One young man was hounded till at last he couldn't get up after a "Lie down!" When he couldn't rise at the command, they kicked him till he fainted. . . . He was completely done, and is still — more than three hours later — lying on the stretcher only half conscious.'

Of these events in their confinement, the CHECKMATE party was only indirectly aware, kept in touch and steadied in fear of their own fate by messages through the air vents explaining each terrifying climax of uproar with its stamping of feet, slamming of doors and raised voices. So violent had daily life become before the heat of July was replaced by a distinctly chilly August, that Nansen was expressing to the senior SS officers his dread of horrors to come if there was not an improvement in relations between staff and prisoners. The extent to which he underestimated the future was fortunate. Had he and all the others been aware of what September and the months to come would bring, he might not only have abandoned all hope, but come also to understand that, in terms of oppression, Grini was but a rest camp.

17

Journey to Purgatory

Stress and tension mounted to new peaks towards the beginning of September as Seidler pursued a vendetta against Nansen by sending him to join the CHECKMATE party in the *Einselhaft*. At the root of it all lay the Commandant's distaste for the Norwegian's prestige within the camp. As the immediate cause, Nansen's involvement with an hilariously funny letter written for the benefit of the Norwegian censor who so enjoyed what he read that he could not bear to part with it—with the result that it fell into German hands. The letter, written in a mixture of Norwegian, Malay, French, English and Dutch to a girl called Anne, and which included miscellaneous vulgarities such as 'Your grandmother was an old Batavian monkey' and 'Kiss my arse you old chimpanzee', had as its theme a plotted mutiny. It revealed that machine-guns, revolvers and radio transmitters, as well as receivers, were hidden throughout the camp and the *Revier*. Incredibly the Germans fell for it. Urgent reports were sent to Oslo and studied there in consternation by the highest authorities. Within the *Einselhaft* punishments rained down upon suspects, all of whom were put on a bread and water diet which had to be supplemented by the stick and sock supply line. Individual guards vied for distinction, the top award for sheer unpleasantness going to a fat lout nicknamed, it seems by the British, Porky—although what 'Porky' Burgess thought of that is not known. For he would have been incapable of rivalling his namesake in the manner of thrusting food into cells, dealing out blows, inflicting harsh physical training and endlessly shouting in the worst form of SS uncouthness. Nobody but a member of the lowest order of SS was capable of that, it was agreed.

The climax was reached shortly after nightfall with the calling of an unscheduled parade, generating fears that something quite unusually dreadful was about to happen when the tables were set up in the centre of the *appelplatz* and the prisoners were ordered to line up before them. From their cell windows, Godwin, Nansen and the others were able to watch the prisoners assembling, hounded by yelping guards. Then, from the gateway, beneath the glare of arclights and additional searchlights, the motor cavalcade entered. First a column of Army soldiers who were efficiently divided into parties and placed under the leadership of SS guards began a search of all the huts and cells.

Next the highest in the land in black Mercedes limousines from which emerged, in due order of seniority, Fehlis and Reinhardt of the SS and at their head none other than Reich Commissioner Terboven in full uniform.

All of a sudden it dawned upon the Norwegians, if not upon the British, what this meant. The Germans really had concluded that a full-scale mutiny was intended and had brought all their guns to bear with awesome ceremony to crush it at source. Visions of a drum-headed court martial followed by executions on the spot loomed up as the search parties thrashed their way from hut to hut and cell to cell, the soldiers looking more and more bored, the guards growing more frenzied and, withall, an all too amazing lack of incriminating material. Amidst this turmoil the CHECKMATE party waited in trepidation, terrified they might be affected, expecting to be called out as the special target for SS hatred—until it occurred to them that this time it was the Norwegians, instead of themselves, who were in hot water. Then, as abruptly as it all had begun, it ended. With nothing but a few stolen vegetables to be shown and the letter all too obviously a hoax, Reich Commissioner Terboven angrily realised that he and his entourage had been made fools of in public and now it was the turn of the SS camp officers to suffer from a verbal lashing before the great man departed, followed by the soldiers whose officers, no doubt, enjoyed a sly smirk at SS discomforture.

The abortive raid had to have its inevitable backlash. Never could the SS afford to stand idly by when made to look foolish. Beatings took place in the *Einselhaft*. At once the transportation programme was accelerated and shaped to include all 'special' and 'difficult' prisoners. First to receive marching orders on 11 September was Godwin and his six followers; mightily relieved at the prospects of a change of scenery and that they were being kept together. Yet scarcely imagining there could be anything ahead much worse than what they had suffered already. Prison life, like any other form of drudgery, is ever at a nadir of existence. The slightest impending change could only, in the minds of the optimistic prisoners, be an improvement on what had gone before. Without optimism there could be no future, only moral and physical deterioration in a slough of degradation.

Travelling by bus to Oslo on the 12th was a wildly exhilarating experience, watching the green countryside roll by and seeing people standing in the fields and the village streets, people who enjoyed freedom—well, a modicum of freedom—was stimulating. They revelled at the sight of Oslo, maybe somewhat tawdry because of war's austerity, yet spacious in its appearance by comparison with the narrow and muddy vista of Grini as surveyed from a cell window. Then, after a few hours despondency when dumped in the prison yard at Akershus, forward again to the quayside, climbing a big ship's gangway under the eyes of soldiers in full battle order crowding the decks above—cannon fodder for the Russian front or for Italy where the Allies were thrusting ahead, gradually closing in upon Germany whence they all were bound. Finally herded below into the hold to find whatever place they could on the deck and snatch a night's sleep, lulled by the homely throb of ship's engines, the first since taking passage on MTB 626—how long ago? Nearly five months! Incredible!

A pity, they thought, if a mine or some lurking submarine's torpedo struck home. Berthed below decks, they would be nearest the explosion, last to reach the lifeboats. On the other hand, there was gladness; a stupendous sense of liberty while under Army, as opposed to SS, custody with the minimum of supervision (who, in any case was likely to attempt an escape at sea?) and without a spate of orders. The rejoicing at no longer being singled out for special treatment. Above all the meals, which were by far the best since captivity and, had they but known it, the best they would ever enjoy while in German custody. Soup with plenty of meat; ample bread with lashings of real butter; coffee and tea of recognisable taste and consistency and all at close intervals, quite unstinted. A dream in every way.

In addition, a vista of 'freedom' off the port bow, when they were allowed on deck as their ship navigated the Kattegat, the lights of Sweden shining in rare contrast to the blackout of most countries in Europe's fifth year of war. Then, far too swiftly, the awakening and return to reality as the passage up the River Oder led to the port of Stettin and a bomb-battered quayside where all too recognisable figures, distinctive with their black collar patches and skull badges, stood waiting, eager to begin the familiar and monotonous ritual of shouting and screaming at their charges as they disembarked. And matching this bankrupt display the utter desolation of the once prosperous port, hammered into a jumble of pulverised buildings by Anglo-American bombers, depopulated except for those, including some French prisoners of war, who worked what was left of the port, and by disinterested knots of aged people, dejected children and cripples.

Travel by rail to a destination said to be Oranienburg proved in keeping with the state of the port. Crammed into dilapidated cattle waggons with extremely rudimentary sanitary facilities, it was discovered that 50 men could not all lie down or sit at once. So for a journey of 100 miles, which took nearly 24 hours, ten at a time had to stand, clinging to anything available to avoid being thrown down. Only once did they stop for soup, the cleaning of the trucks and for a brief stretching of legs—a most welcome interlude and interesting, too. For the station was the Anhalter, in Berlin, set amidst the damage caused by bombing and containing a gathering of mute German civilians who stared through the prisoners as if they were invisible. As never before the CHECKMATE party and the Norwegians came to understand what was meant by discerning Germans who admitted that their race had 'ceased to think'. Apparently they had also forgotten, in the mass, to feel. Or was it a sense of shame? Or apathy, the product of terror?

Exactly what this meant in terms of compassion was still more precisely illustrated when the train halted at Sachsenhausen station and, stiff and sore, the prisoners piled out onto the platform to be greeted by the customary chorus of shouting SS—plus something fresh in their experience. First an unknown class of guard, poorly clad and unhealthy in looks, who, it turned out, were inmates of the concentration camp for which they were bound. Known as Kapots and employed under the duress of SS terror, it was their fate to do the SS's work, to copy them in excesses of mannerisms and brutality for fear of the consequences to themselves. Second, excited spectators, a crowd of children equipped with wooden machine-guns which they aimed at the prisoners (as they must have done on many previous occasions), making tat-tat-tat noises with practised aggression and throwing stones for good measure.

As so often they had done in moments of depression since their capture and on the rail journey from Stettin, the prisoners had sung, Godwin, Burgess and the others taking a lead which the Norwegians eagerly took up. They sang, too, on the march from the station to the camp, but their voices faltered when they caught sight of their destination. Founded on thin Prussian sand amid scrupulously tended Prussian ever-dark forests stood the camp, its name emblazoned on the wall—*Sachsenhausen Schutschaftlager*; its inmates clad in the blue-striped, shapeless prison uniform, toiling listlessly on either side of the approach road, which ran alongside a seemingly endless electrified wire fence to the gateway at the far side.

The welcome in the reception hut advertised camp methods. Here the Kapots, called that because they alone wore caps and about 50 per cent of whom were themselves prisoners, subjected the new intake to the ponderous induction process which typified the rotten inefficiency of a system long since culled of initiative. To begin with, the cleansing of each man as he was told to strip naked and hand in all his personal clothing and effects before fumigation as a precaution against lice and the ever-present threat, in overcrowded living accommodation, of typhus. Next, shearing at the hands of barbers who seemed to have learnt their trade at an abattoir and who, by a single light bulb, removed every trace of hair from head and body by the minimum possible strokes of electric cutters which left many prisoners cut and bleeding. Then the showering in water which was alternately scalding hot or freezing cold, followed by annointment with a repulsive anti-lice cream. Finally, fitting out with prison clothing which apparently was designed to neutralise the entire cleansing operation. For almost every item of ragged and rough underwear, socks and the ill-fitting, thin, blue-striped uniforms were filthy, seemingly the unwashed hand-me-downs of prisoners who, no doubt, had fallen victim to the camp's rigours. Already indeed it was evident that the mortality rate was high. Norwegians who had long been present came to meet old friends and, in the jargon of the place, listed those who had 'lost their pep' and 'gone up the chimney', illustrating the smoke of the crematorium with a circular, upward movement of the hand.

It took several hours for the new arrivals to go through and emerge as convicts, a time in which the CHECKMATE party stoically awaited segregation into the solitary confinement they expected in conformity with their 'special status'. It was not to be. They were treated like the other Norwegians and in due course found themselves among a group which had completed documentation, led through chill air which swiftly penetrated their worthless clothing and directed into a hut filled with three-tiered bunks and packed to the limit with men.

The psychological impact of Sachsenhausen upon the tens of thousands who passed through it have been variously recorded, a testimony of initial astonishment and despair, a catalogue of iniquity compiled by strong-minded survivors. Godwin at once recognised in its system the greatest challenge yet to his leadership, and his six followers automatically looked to him for guidance while trying to find their feet in a foreign environment. As a prime aim, in addition to learning the camp routine and discovering the numerous tricks of the local trade, Godwin had to re-establish the group feeling which had lapsed somewhat during the months of imprisonment. Grini had divided them into pairs which had rarely been able to communicate between each other. Cox with Burgess, Hiscock with Mayor and Roe with West. He feared they might have suffered from more than physical decline, concerned that their fighting spirit and will to win might have been weakened from lack of his own leadership. In this he was largely wrong. The fact was that each of his men was a leader and perfectly aware of the demands of survival. As a first priority, therefore, he could concentrate upon jointly learning the camp rules, tightening up their liaison with the Norwegians among whom they were, thankfully, billetted and, with the least delay (subject to the food and opportunity available), restoring their strength and fitness to the level at which it had stood when they left Lerwick on this ill-fated mission.

PLATE 16.   Godwin and captor at Haugesund before the interrogations began

PLATE 17.   SS man shouting at Grini working party (by Odd Nansen)

PLATE 18.   Musselmen at Sachsenhausen looking for scraps from the Norwegian table (by Odd Nansen)

PLATE 19.   Norwegian Christmas at Sachsenhausen (by Odd Nansen)

18

'Work Makes Free'

Sachsenhausen *Schutschaftlager*, as those who lived long enough might learn, had been founded in 1933 shortly after Hitler came to power. Its purpose was to detain, often without trial, those who were opposed to the Nazi regime, people such as members of the Social Democratic and the Communist Parties as well as staunch dissidents of the calibre of Pastor Niemoller. Constructed in a huge circle, with huts radiating from a large central parade ground, its original capacity was for about 10,000 prisoners. Because of its close proximity to Berlin as well as the SS Headquarters set up by Heinrich Himmler at Oranienburg, it was the natural choice as a showpiece for display to visiting foreigners and journalists to see for themselves that concentration camps were run in an orderly and humane manner and were merely a temporary expedient during the initial phase of the German revolution. The facilities installed in Sachsenhausen, such as an extremely well-equipped hospital, were therefore of an unusually high standard, better than those of the other camps dotted about Germany. But this began to change for the worse when, in 1939, the original Adjutant, Rudolf Hoess, became Commandant.

It was Hoess's brief to strengthen the system in association with what was already the SS's pronounced taste for extermination of undesirable species and to enhance the exploitation of concentration camps as sources of cheap labour. Under Hoess (who, in 1940, was to set up at Auschwitz, the first extermination camp), the dilution of the hard-core SS Kapots with prisoners and, later, a high proportion of foreigners, went hand in glove with security measures encouraging SS to inform on SS, as well as anybody else in or outside the prison communities. To join the original political detainees, many of whom were of the highest integrity and intelligence and who were bitterly opposed to Nazi ideology and methods, came the scum of Germany—psychopaths, thieves, murderers, perverts of every conceivable kind. And to supervise them, professional criminals of all trades who dealt exclusively in corruption and terror and to whom sympathy and kindness were rejected qualities. Under this influence, the camp's conditions worsened as efficiency declined, as the numbers held steadily increased and as the cruelties inflicted upon the prisoners, without necessarily killing them except in severe instances of felony, became legion.

Hoess's successor recognised that matters had gone too far. The camp was becoming a quagmire of iniquity and almost unmanageable. The most depraved of the guards were drafted to units such as the special extermination squads (*sonderkommandos*) operating in the occupied territories of the East, and to anti-partisan formations like the infamous Dirlewanger Regiment, whose atrocities were merely frowned upon, and where their peculiar talents could be employed to the full but under warped SS discipline. This cleansing of the Sachsenhausen ranks barely improved matters. The rot was too deeply rooted for eradication, especially since the replacement SS were mainly social and career failures who were incapable of coping even with normality, let alone an expanding organisation lacking a code of decency.

SS factory complexes were being built adjacent to the camps to be manned by an influx of prisoners from the conquered territories. Very shortly Godwin became aware that Sachsenhausen's prison population stood at about 17,000 and, in addition to being employed as guards and in agriculture and forestry, working in, among several places, a factory making signals equipment (which also acted as a useful source of supply for clandestine radio sets) and a boot and shoe factory, of which Himmler was a Director. A manifestation of the shoe factory was on display for some ten hours a day, seven days a week—a figure-of-eight trackway within the camp around which trudged the so-called *Schuprüfungskommando*. Here recalcitrant prisoners were driven, under close surveillance, to march 48 kilometres a day testing the products of the factory in all conditions. Yet in a camp where discipline was enforced with blatant harshness under the lash and by public executions, this was a special punishment system of a comparatively sophisticated nature and for periods of only a week or two at a time.

In crowding reminiscent of the rescuing destroyer after the sinking of *Ark Royal*, Godwin found himself rubbing shoulders with a cross-section of Europe's people—Czechs, Russians, Slovaks, Ukrainians, Poles, Frenchmen, members of the Luxembourg Royal Guard (who had refused to join the German Army and, like the CHECKMATE party, had lost their prisoner-of-war status), Germans, Belgians, Dutchmen and Norwegians. Each nationality occupied its regulated place in the social scale as ordained by German dictates and governed by rules of 'prominence'. Lowest in the order rotted the much despised Ukrainians who were treated as dirt, given the most menial tasks and were so impoverished and starved of food that they were doomed to become walking skeletons, known as *Die Musselmänner* (Musselmen). Highest in the order stood *Die Prominenten*, those of purest racial standing (in German eyes) who filled the best camp jobs and enjoyed friendships of influence. Top among the *prominenten* were Nordic people—the Norwegians and, in a minority of only seven, the British CHECKMATE party whose close integration with the Norwegians won for them a measure of preferential treatment—to begin with. And in a category of their own, a few Jews, balancing between life and eternity.

The Norwegians ruled because of another vital reason. Among their number were to be found the most brilliant of the younger generation, including scholars and future politicians. It was said that future governments of Norway were formed in embryo in Sachsenhausen. The task of the leaders with social conscience was extremely hard and painful. In a class society of high degree in which each individual was compelled by the conditions to cling to life through his own personal ingenuity, along with dextrous involvement with his particular group, there was but little latitude for philanthropy.

The Musselmen picked up scraps from the tables of the other European nations. The Norwegians enjoyed comparative plenty, notably because they alone were receiving food parcels from outside, from the neutral Scandinavian countries, Sweden and Denmark, who looked after their own and kept Red Cross supplies moving to the end. Without once asking for charity or privilege, the British were made welcome at the Norwegian table and appointed to work in the kitchen, a plum job since it gave access to sources of food but where, nevertheless, waste food was so scarce that the rat population was starved and hardly noticeable.

Food was the main topic of discussion and the dominant subject with the foremost place in everybody's minds. With only two meals a day of a content less even than that supplied at Grini, the pangs of hunger and the anxieties about where the next meal would come from were continuous. For the first time since Operation CRACKERS, Godwin and West faced up to the agonies and debilitation of malnutrition, the worst effects of which were constantly to be seen among the Musselmen. Had it not been for what they could steal and smuggle from the kitchen, plus the extras of jam, cheese, sugar, meat, fish and special nutrients from the Red Cross parcels, their condition would have deteriorated along with that of the underprivileged prisoners. So when rumours about a ban upon the transport of parcels gained currency, the profoundest despondency fell upon the Norwegians—until it was later announced that this did not include parcels from abroad. Subsisting slightly above the threshold of starvation, the British actually put on a little weight and gained enough energy to enable them to take serious exercise, to rebuild their fitness and sharpen their mental reactions.

This was a heaven-sent interlude within hell, and recognised by Godwin at its face value. Ever the optimist, he was realist enough to visualise a progressive decline in camp conditions with Germany's downward slide into oblivion. Their work in the cookhouse was by no means exacting. There was time in the evenings for sports and games, including a series of 'international' soccer matches which proved amusing and gave West and Burgess their first and only opportunity to play for their country. Indeed, they reached international stardom as members of an Allied XI, until the evening, that is, when they defeated an Axis XI, to the immense displeasure of the Germans who at once put a stop to that sort of contest for ever. In spare moments Godwin had them toning up their muscles with exercises and hardening their feet by jog trotting. He pointed to foundering people, even a few better fed Norwegians among them, and explained that their mental decay was due partly to physical unfitness. 'A tough situation needs tough men, you all know that! So—running on the spot begin! Sergeant Cox, take over!'

They would laugh, knowing it was common sense. Later they might wonder if their officer possessed some sort of crystal ball tucked away.

Sometimes they enjoyed themselves. Distractions were essential and the Norwegians loved to arrange entertainments whenever possible. At Grini they used to hold a cabaret in the church. In Sachsenhausen they did what they could in the huts, and Godwin is remembered for his acts, including an amusing rendering of 'Drink to me only with thine eyes', while the rest of the British joined in strongly with raucous choruses. To both prisoners and prison staff, music was important. As in all the 'best' concentration camps, there was an orchestra, forty-strong with top class musicians. So the classics would be heard along with popular melodies, bawdy songs and the marches sung by prisoners on their way to and from work, or by the *Schuprüfungskommando* tramping out their sentence on the dreary figure-of-eight circuit.

Sachsenhausen survivors tend mainly to recall notorious horrors amid a sea of horror in which the likelihood of mutilation or death lurked constantly at their elbows. They were forced to witness so many floggings—'25 on the arse' as it was known for minor misdemeanours—and so many hangings that it took something personal or exceptionally bizarre to imprint it permanently upon their memories. If a friend was maltreated or killed, that registered; just as did one notorious hanging of a Pole whose feet continued to touch the ground after the drop and he was allowed to writhe and struggle in his bonds while the guards, with callous disregard, called for a shovel and dug a hole for his feet to swing free. No: it was the memories of long hours standing on the *appelplatz* in all sorts of weather, being counted (and recounted when the numbers did not tally); of the perennial discomfiture of hunger; of the utter weariness from lack of sleep brought on by the long hours and overwork; and the racketeering which stuck.

Trade in Sachsenhausen of all commodities was by favour and barter. Services might be paid for by 'presents' of morsels of food or some carefully hoarded luxury item. *Die Prominenten* controlled the highest purchasing power; the rest were reduced to parasites who subserviently attempted to eke out a wage of 6 Reichmarks per day in the factories, less 30 pfennigs maintenance, by stealing and scrounging. Godwin and his men compared notes on ways to earn their keep, to protect their meagre property and to improve their lot. Apart from food, they did manage, as winter cold increased, to acquire warmer clothing by retrieving their uniforms and oilskins. With Norwegian friends—and by now close personal friendships were springing up—they banded together for mutual protection, forging strong bonds of integrity which rarely failed. Somehow, they managed to create centres of semi-order amid the chaos, while waging a losing battle against the filth which surrounded them with its almost total moratorium upon the washing of clothing, bedding and the huts' interiors.

Who could have been the cynic, it was asked, who had composed the maxim decorating the end gables of several huts?

'There is only one road to freedom. Its mile stones are Honesty, Truthfulness, Obedience, Industry, Temperance, Cleanliness and Love of the Fatherland.'

What sort of freedom was envisaged? The realist might answer none at all, as the hard incoming winter, ravaged by remorselessly worsening conditions and intensified brutality by the guards, was softened only by news of continuing Allied successes and heavy air raids which, in their turn, exacerbated the guards' rage and vengeance. But what happened prior to 18 November, terrible as it all was, would be looked back on merely as an overture when a truly spectacular air raid struck Berlin that night with concentrated fury.

19

The Long March

The decision which fundamentally changed the CHECKMATE party's way of life was taken miles away in mid-November, in London, and at Bentley Priory, High Wycombe. When the Air Officer Commanding Bomber Command, Air Marshal Sir Arthur Harris, put forward a plan to make Germany sue for peace, he submitted a paper to the War Cabinet on 3 November, stating his conviction that the combined efforts of the British and US Air Forces could wreck Berlin from end to end, at a cost, he thought, of 400–500 bombers, and that Germany must then collapse. How Harris and his colleagues came to the conclusion that Germany's morale would break was somewhat obscure and need not be discussed here. But assuredly, in assessing the power of Hitler's government and the State over his people's minds, insufficient account was taken of the insidious grip of the SS and the *Wehrmacht* upon almost every element of German society. Given the opportunity, the prisoners of Sachsenhausen might have been able to explain how it was that the police state system operated through brutish control and the inculcation of mutual suspicion at all levels. But even then it is to be doubted if leaders in Britain who had never experienced anything like it could have imagined its effects. As it was, the Intelligence reports only hinted at German subservience to fearsome pressures.

Berliners took cover on the night of 18 November and, for the umpteenth time, heard the guns bark, the thunder of engines from hundreds of aircraft and the whine and crash of bombs pounding their city into rubble. At Sachsenhausen, in accordance with the normal procedure, the lights were extinguished and the prisoners ordered to their huts where they went to bed in the dark. No shelter for them in thick concrete bunkers or deep cellars, as the majority of German citizens used in Berlin and surrounding towns and villages. But a high degree of risk from bombs cast down by errant aircraft or from unexploded shells as nearby gun batteries opened up against waves of raiders rolling in for an hour without a break, lighting the sky with flares and the glow of fires.

Night after night the hooters blared and everybody cowered. Frequently very little happened, because only a handful of raiders came over to keep the Germans—and the prisoners—in tension and short of sleep. But when the

126

bombers swarmed over in their hundreds on the nights of 22, 23 and 26 November, and again on 2 December, the effect on morale, as expressed in conflicting emotions of terror, horror of man's torment of man, in exultation at the punishment being inflicted upon the Germans, or in fury against those who inflicted it, was traumatic. Some among the prisoners endeavoured, unsuccessfully, to close their senses to the bombardment. Others watched through the hut windows and gave vivid running commentaries, interspersed with cheers when flames leapt up, or groans when a bomber was picked out overhead by a German fighter and fell to ground. A few, so weary as to be numb, actually managed to sleep through a nearby bomber crash. Among the most delighted and vocal were Godwin and his men whose hatred of the Germans by now matched that of the longest suffering European under the SS heel.

Within hours of the second strong raid, the inmates of Sachsenhausen were witness to the fate of some among Berlin's weaker-minded or more sensitive citizens. As rumours were heard of an Allied ultimatum, calling upon the Germans to surrender on pain of being bombed to extinction, several score bewildered and terrified Berliners were herded through the gates and shortly to the *Industriehof* to be shot. They were either looters or defeatists, it was said. In practical terms, they were examples displayed as a deterrent to anybody else who might feel the slightest temptation to bend to enemy intent—victims of a crackdown by the SS and the Army as they took control in the battered and burning city. Small wonder that foreign observers, finding resignation among their contacts, repeatedly used the word 'apathy' when reporting upon the German people's outlook. All the more reason why the arbiters of oppression should feel free to indulge in retribution.

To SS officers of the Special Commission responsible to Himmler for the Sachsenhausen complex, *Standartenführer* Kaindl, *Untersturmführer* Hohne and *Obersturmführer* Cornelius, at least one of whom had a family and property in Berlin, the nearest most obvious target for reprisals was the British group. It was a target, moreover, which was being brought increasingly to their attention because of certain inquiries and pertinent questions being raised by the British government through international channels as to the whereabouts and welfare of the seven British sailors. On or about 8 December they struck. All seven British were called out from their hut and marched away to the separate fenced enclosure allocated to the *Schuprüfungskommando*—generally known in camp, as now it will be here, as the SK—once referred to by Nansen as 'a slow form of capital punishment'.

In huts 13 and 14, Godwin found conditions which were far worse than those in the Norwegian billets. Each hut was divided into two by a central lavatory and an office, packed with up to 45 men of several nationalities who had been picked out for punishment. Rows of three-tiered bunks, separated by narrow passages, filled the dormitories. On the bunks lay filthy mattresses, filled with wood wool, a skimpy pillow and a horse blanket.

Stealing—or 'organising' as it was better known—was far more rife among this mixed and regularly changing community than with the Norwegians. Every article had to be watched constantly and at night, when asleep, each man hid his possessions inside the mattress and kept his boots under the pillow. Otherwise, next morning, they would be gone, as currency to buy food. Reveille would take place at between 4 and 5 o'clock to the accompaniment of shouts, screams and obscenities from the Kapots who might lash out at anybody slow to hit the floor. By dim lighting, the prisoners would wash in cold water at the concrete stand with space for only 12–14 at once, would make their beds and then parade outside. The time permitted was short and bedmaking by inhabitants of the top tiers extremely difficult.

Each morning, seven days a week, the scene was the same, the darkness of the *appelplatz* swept by searchlights as nearly 20,000 pyjama-striped human beings stumbled into line, goaded by the boots and sticks of screaming Kapots. It was like something out of Pandemonium, to which the SK were distinctly underprivileged spectators, isolated as they were in their own peculiar hell. Counting and inspection, followed by a sharp dose of physical training, would precede an abysmally thin soup breakfast and the day's monotonous labour.

Some prisoners might waste an hour or more each day in the trek to their workplace. For the SK, the figure-of-eight trackway was next door to the *appelplatz*, built of successive sections composed of asphalt, cobbles, gravel, sand, soil, cement and an expanse of water 5 cm deep. Clad in a variety of numbered boots and shoes (occasionally women's shoes, although these the British were never made to wear), they would start marching, each kilometre carefully registered by a supervisor, until 48 kilometres (30 miles)—no more and no less—had been covered. Then the boots, often made of experimental synthetic materials and fishskin, besides ordinary leather, were taken away for examination and repair at night by Russian prisoners, in readiness for the next day's march.

Ordinarily a prisoner consigned to the SK would serve one or two, at most four, weeks undergoing this exacting exercise upon which doubling and press-ups were sometimes superimposed by way of assuaging the guard's whims. Extra punishments were the rule rather than the exception. He who stumbled or could not keep up the pace might be kicked and beaten into insensibility. Some would be removed to the *Industriehof* and shot. A few committed suicide by hanging themselves. Many just died in misery.

Strong as they were, Godwin and his companions reckoned they could last out until Christmas time, in the expectation that they would then be sent back among their Norwegian friends. In the meantime, it had to be faced that they might be driven deliberately into failure as a subtle way of executing them without recourse to questionable legal procedures and the bullet. This was when Godwin's insistence upon physical fitness paid off by cushioning the initial shock of the gruelling course. In bracing them to the perils of the future, he had, with prescience, foreseen a spell in the SK, just as he foresaw still more terrifying ordeals to come. The food which continued to be provided by Norwegians, who went on caring about the British as if they were of their own people, ensured the maintenance of stamina. After each day's wearisome slog, the British visited their friends to share the food parcels, savour the remarkably tasty dishes concoted by their hosts' chefs, and be stimulated by the latest news and the lively conversation of intellectuals.

Visiting outside the SK compound was, of course, a breach of the rules, and the passage through wire and across open spaces made especially hazardous because the British, quite literally, were marked men. The large E sewn to their striped clothing had to be hidden under uniform jackets, worn on top. To be caught was to qualify for one of the severer punishments awarded, such as '25 on the arse' while face downwards on the so-called *Schlägerbank*. To begin with, visits were fairly haphazard due to inexperience and on the assumption that they might not be kept for long in the SK. Rapidly they became expert, under instruction from Jack Cox, in commando methods of patrolling and the penetration of wire barricades, of moving unimpeded about the camp after dark. More slowly it dawned upon them that their fate was linked to reprisals connected to the RAF raids and that they might be permanently posted to the SK. Over the next 3½ months there would be 12 severe night raids on Berlin by the RAF and, in March 1944, four large-scale daylight attacks by the US Air Force—interspersed with 16 minor raids by small, harassing forces. In fact, there were very few nights when the sirens did not sound. As a result, the initial thought, 'Oh, well! If we're in the SK to satisfy SS bloodymindedness, maybe when the raids stop they'll think again', came to be replaced by a grim realisation that bloodymindedness had come to stay.

As part of the Christmas festivities, which the Norwegians with their British guests celebrated as best they could in decorated huts, with national flags on the tables, a special meal, readings and singing, the Germans planted a candle-lit tree where the *appelplatz* gallows (called Tyburn by the Norwegians) was usually erected. And next day the SK, with the British among them, were back on the road, marching the full 30 miles without the slightest hint of the end being in sight.

When it became plain that remission was to be denied them, and that, apparently, they were doomed, like the Flying Dutchman, to travel until they broke, Godwin let his men know what he expected of them:

'We are not going to be licked this way by Hitler and his blackguards. I know it looks as if they're out to kill us by degrees like so many poor chaps, and we are sunk if the Norwegians don't stick by us. Well I'm as sure as is possible they will stand by us, if not from pure humanity out of determination to put one over on the SS. What I feel is, that it's up to us to hang on, not to let them grind us down. What's 30 miles a day, after all if we can keep up our strength? We've been at it for nearly three weeks already and the war's not going to last for ever. So what I'm saying is, let's show the bastards, for ourselves, our families and for King and country, we can take it.'

An appeal of that persuasive power was guaranteed to catch their imaginations; men to whom patriotism was part of life, drummed into them at home, at school and in the conventional propaganda of the period. The major problem, henceforward and in addition to obtaining sufficient nourishment, was to defeat the Sachsenhausen system by overcoming boredom during the monotonous daily round, avoiding the worst excesses of punishments awarded and getting enough sleep despite the nightly roar of air raids, guards and prisoners. As individuals, unsupported, they would have been doomed by loneliness in a hostile environment. But as a team, with Godwin's example of supreme leadership, they had a chance. By cajolery, pleading, bullying and his own unwavering performance and sheer force of personality, he managed to inspire them. In return, they responded from out of the disciplines of the military system, from personal and national pride and sheer common sense in the realisation that this might be the key to survival. They held their backs that much straighter, made that extra effort to keep themselves clean and tidy despite every obstacle (including the poor quality hard soap provided) against them. And the Norwegians in amazement, when watching from their own pit of despair, took courage by regarding the British as an emblem of resistance, and made it a matter of honour as well as of humanity to go on providing sustenance to the British who, in return, looked upon the Norwegians as an anchor to civilisation.

Now it was that the knowledge and experience of Sergeant Cox was put to its full use, he who had once almost blighted his future as a commando by falling out from a 100-mile forced march. Cox it was who pointed out, after the first four days, that they had completed 120 miles; he who taught them to overcome the mental as well as the physical torments of a long march through controlled effort and devious psychological diversions. How to relax the muscles and shut the mind to the immediate surroundings by conjuring up images of pleasanter journeys back home. At any one moment he might, in his mind's eye, be walking to Yeovil from North Cadbury for a visit to the cinema; Godwin striding the range in Argentina; West sauntering down Argyle Street from the Central Station; Mayor strolling the banks of the Ribble; Burgess the pathways along the canal from Beverley to Thearne; Roe the streets of London's West End and Hiscock the coast road from Trinity to Port Poxton. It was a grand illusion designed to keep them sane, maintain their resolve, pitching out of plain bloodymindedness to defeat German iniquity and inhumanity—a vivid contest of Good against Evil watched over by an audience which could not afford to be dispassionate.

They also sang. How they sang! There are Norwegians who remember them most for the memory that they were always singing, day after day, week after week and month after month as Christmas Day with its carols past and the New Year dawned as prologue to a 1944 of air raids and vanishing hope as they were kept in the SK. Odd Nansen recorded the pious carols booming over the loudspeakers while SS soldiers in steel helmets, tommy guns and machine-guns 'stood ready at the least sign to shatter the darkness and Christmas peace with bellowing and bullets'. And the camp orchestra playing as if its life depended upon it (as it may well have done) '. . . a whole section of Grieg. The whole Peer Gynt suite. Not as it should be played; but still it was Grieg and it was music. For a moment one could forget oneself.' Different from the tunes Godwin and Burgess led them in singing on the march—anything from old music hall tunes, regimental marches and lewd ballards, about such unhappy men as *The One Eyed Riley*, to *Onward Christian Soldiers*—but uplifting just the same. And as with so much else, in defiance of the SS who, in subtle ways by the right people, could be defied.

Blockälteste Jakob, the Kapot in charge of the SK, sometimes tried to dictate what was sung—for singing on the march is among the traditions of the German Army. He preferred German battle songs and once, as Arne Herwander recalls:

> ' . . . told us to sing a Norwegian song. We immediately started to sing good old *Tipperary*. . . . They got quite mad and sent those of us who had British uniforms to the tailors . . . to cut off our shoulder straps and make holes in our tunics, overcoats and trousers. Coloured patches were attached and yellow stripes were painted on the uniforms and caps.'

The slightest misdemeanour brought its punishment. Frequently Godwin would assume the blame for trivial faults by his men and take the punishment. Yet apart from beatings and execution, how much more could *Lagerälteste* Kunke or any German inflict? Well, one way was to make them carry up to 40 lb extra on their backs and chests when marching. Which inspired a song, words by Godwin:

> When we are marching around the *appelplatz*
> Leather boots and tiddly hats
> That's where the boys are doing their best, Cox and West.
> You can hear the hell bell ring, with a ding aling aling,
> When we are marching around the *appelplatz*, with the gang.
> Now the Foreman said to me as I turned up rather late,
> You had better *Pass mal auf*, or you will be standing at the gate.
> *Halt die snause blode hund*, or you will be carrying forty pound,
> when we are marching around the *appelplatz* with the gang.
> But now hear said I to him, I don't like your tone,
> If you don't like our marching you had better send us home.
> *Halt die snause blode hund*, or you will be carrying forty pound.
> When we are marching around the *appelplatz* with the gang.

Each of them in his turn would suffer from spells of depression when the treadmill looked never-ending or in a waking hour at night amid rancid squalor of the overcrowded hut, or when some poor devil was strung up before their eyes, or when the brutal Kunke was behaving at his most bestial. It was almost impossible to shut the mind to it, try as they would to divert their thoughts into various channels. Of the youngsters, Mayor and Burgess 'celebrated' their 21st birthdays there (West having genuinely celebrated his only three days before they set out from Lerwick). It was impossible to do much to make the day any different from those which dragged on before or after; but they tried with small gifts, hearty congratulations and the wish, as a prayer, that next year they would all be celebrating anniversaries at home. Their yearnings centred constantly on their families and those at home. As for prayer, that was a private matter, but each prayed in his own way at moments of terror, or depression, or when it was possible in the loneliness of the night to achieve a moment of calm composure. Each endured his own private hell. Doubtless Alfred Roe, the only married one among them, suffered most as he worried for his wife. Sometimes, maybe, the ratings cursed Godwin under their breath for his relentless determination to keep them going. But keep going they did.

The CHECKMATE party had a sight of camp life denied to most other prisoners, because they spent all day at its centre while the rest mostly worked elsewhere. It was common knowledge, of course, that 'to stand at the gate' was to reach the final staging post prior to be marched outside, wheeled to the right and 'transported', as the term was, to the execution place adjacent to the crematorium. But so long as that remained only a threat, they were able to watch the SS going about their daily work, and gauge the effect of events of world moment upon their despised and hated oppressors. When the Allies landed at Anzio, ripples of SS alarm were soon followed by triumphant crowing when the attack stalled and Rome did not fall—as had so confidently been expected. Daylight raids by American heavy bombers on four occasions in March against Berlin—the first time this had been attempted—disrupted the camp's schedule, even that of the SK, as the sirens blared and the rumble of hundreds of engines from on high struck fear into all who heard it and watched. On the last of these daylight visits bombs fell miles from the Berlin target, but hitting a military objective by straddling the SS quarters and factory buildings and scoring a hit on a prison hut. Buildings and machinery burned nicely, although the casualties, by some miracle, were extremely light, the only confirmed death being that of a Ukrainian shot on the spot for stealing a loaf of bread from the ruins. Allied successes frequently had their adverse aspect. When considerable damage was done by American bombers in daylight on 18 April to the Heinkel factory close by, a great many prisoners were killed and injured. With mixed feelings the prisoners watched the 'superb spectacle' of the fighting overhead, a bomber in flames and its crew parachuting to earth and the rush of bombs, the roar of enormous explosions and the smoke and flames filling the atmosphere; also the rarity of being told, at one factory, to take cover in nearby shelters only to be thrown out by the SS cowering there whose proper duty it was to be up above coping with the emergency.

Good news from the battle fronts by far outstripped bad, which was increasingly rare. The fall of Rome, filtering through on 5 June, provided a sparkling aperitif to the vintage announcement at noon next day of the start of the long awaited Second Front. As news of the Allied landings in Normandy broke, the camp's populace erupted, each in its own way. SS officers flung open doors to shout among themselves and boasted that at last the decisive day had dawned with the impending defeat of the Anglo-American forces, proof that Germany's final victory was inevitable. But this was prisoners' day, as the normal routine, even that of the SK, was interrupted by the sensation, as friends communicated the news with congratulations as fast as possible to the CHECKMATE party who had a special vested interest in an invasion of which they, over a year previously, had been the tip of the spearhead. Now everybody, in addition to the British whose smiles and songs were always on display as a sign of their invincibility, was whistling, singing, joking, enwrapped in a mood of gaiety which no amount of German boasting, about colossal losses inflicted or the annihilation of enemy parachute formations, could extinguish.

As a matter of course, the SS reacted violently to an event which even they could not disguise as a fundamental change of circumstances. Combined with a sudden and amazingly deferred urge to eliminate the officially permitted Communist influence in the camp, they began degrading and removing the senior Germans of that party who for years had held key positions as block leaders, as well as Kapot assistants. Men who, at unguarded moments, might admit to the British and Norwegians their resolve, on the day of reckoning, to obliterate the Nazi SS with a ferocity akin to that being employed against German Communists were now eliminated in their turn. In the place of the deposed returned an old anarchy, the gangsters and criminals of a type previously favoured by the evil Hoess. Henceforward, 'organising' would flourish with unprecedented criminality as the lip service to legality which, overall, had retained a façade of propriety over SS depradations was quelled. Punishments would be awarded with abandon and insensate direction, often on the spur of the moment, increasingly with fatal consequences. Accountability was reduced to a premium. No man's life was safe and might easily be ended summarily, at whim.

Far more threatening, the SS showed signs of decreasing confidence in themselves, after the unsuccessful attempt upon the life of their revered Führer on 20 July opened a new chapter in their lives. The pep talks to the camp staff by senior officers exposed an underlying concern at loss of faith in the ultimate triumph of National Socialism. The trials of the conspirators who had dared try to kill Hitler, and the horrifying death that some of them met, hung by piano wire, suspended from hooks in the ceiling, was but one method of indicating that nobody who resisted the Thousand Year Reich would receive clemency. Yet not entirely successful in re-establishing the belief of those who had committed themselves to the depths of evil and knew that, in defeat, they might be brought to trial for their crimes. Threats were to be heard during Allied radio broadcasts to which the SS listened. Meanwhile, the leaders were being addressed as directly as possible by the British government through the established neutral channels, mainly via Switzerland and Sweden. At a time when the leaders of the SS were turning their thoughts to covering their tracks in the postwar world by eradicating evidence of their acts, messages were being received which had a direct bearing upon Godwin and his men.

At the beginning of April 1944 positive information from a Norwegian was received in London that the CHECKMATE party had been transferred from Grini to Germany. Until then all attempts to obtain an admission from the Germans of the party's existence had failed—and would continue to be ignored. Already, however, the British government had made it clear that it was well informed about the treatment accorded to prisoners wearing British uniform who, contrary to the Geneva Convention of 1929, had been '. . . captured by the German Armed Forces on or off the Norwegian Coast and have been shot in cold blood'. And on at least two occasions, in February and October 1944, had

> 'demanded an immediate assurance that the strictest instructions have been issued . . . that all personnel of the British Armed Forces or Allied Forces under British Command captured in the course of Military Operations who are wearing Naval, Military or Air Force Uniform shall be accorded the full rights and privileges of Prisoners of War to which they are entitled under the rules of war and the provisions of International Law.'

Still the German legal departments minuted that there was no proven case of sabotage against the British party. Still the party marched day after day in the SK. On 6 June, when the rejoicing about the Second Front was at its height, they had completed 178 days, a total of 5340 miles. By then they had become experts in marching techniques and cunning in steering clear of trouble and winning advantages. They were also a camp institution, regarded with awe and admiration by all who watched them smiling their way through the ordeal; even respected by the SS who must have realised how the sailors were being sustained but who were slower to recognise the feat as a threat to themselves. Within the SK, and in the running of its two huts, they naturally acquired what few privileges existed and were looked up to as leaders and supreme advisers. As of right, each slept on one of the best lower bunks and to some extent managed to control the behaviour of SS victims who came and went. There were limits to this, some of them due to communication difficulties, some to the clash of national characteristics, several to breaches of discipline and not a few to moral collapse. Alf Aadnoy, a member of the Norwegian *prominenten*, who eventually arranged supplies to the Norwegian-run camp hospital, recalled walking close by the trackway one day, to be saluted, as usual with a grin, by Godwin who also pointed to a pair of Germans sharing the march with them that day. 'Germans', he said, raising his eyes to the skies in disdain. And there they were, loudly bickering and squabbling between themselves, disrupting the normally settled routine of the march with its helpful singing.

In their second winter at Sachsenhausen, the camp population swelled as a horde of refugees, evacuated from the Eastern Front before the almost unchecked Russian advance, poured in. It was among the phenomena of Nazi Germany that while leaving to the enemy thousands of its fighting men and masses of war equipment, it sedulously attempted to save a horde of displaced people for recalcitrant labour, along with the contents of the factories they operated so inefficiently and unwillingly. The quality of food declined in conjunction with orders forbidding anybody to give scraps to anybody from Eastern Europe were issued. As Anglo-American armies reached the German frontier in September, the number of prisoners passed the 30,000 mark at the same time as the death rate from pulmonary diseases—pneumonia was the commonest cause of death through malnutrition—steadily rose. Smoke from the crematorium on the opposite side of the wire fence to the hospital belched thicker and for longer periods with every day that passed. Amid filth and overcrowding, the louse problem loomed up, with the fight to prevent typhus largely frustrated by a quota of just one shower a week and no means to wash ragged clothing.

On 5 October, Odd Nansen recorded an outbreak of typhus with 23 cases, one of them in a Norwegian hut. Fortunately it was contained, but it served a warning that not even the Germans dared ignore, yet they too were defeated by the continued arrival of more prisoners from the East, raising the camp total to about 50,000—nobody quite knew how many. The majority were infested and already walking skeletons, who were virtually incapable of caring for themselves. Suspicion and terror radiated throughout the camp as the Nazi leaders at last came to recognise their days in power were numbered. Once that became apparent, it would be every SS man for himself. A number of snap arms-searches of prisoners were enacted and the removal of possible rivals among the prison guards commenced. To the delight of Godwin, the rest of the SK and those Norwegians who had suffered under his hand, *Lagerälteste* Kunke was demoted, humiliated by receiving at least twice the statutory '25 on the arse' he had inflicted on others, and transported to an unannounced fate. But still there was the huge *Blockälteste* Jakob, an Army deserter whose only hope of expiation rested on his ability to satisfy superiors by behaving more outrageously with boot and stick than the rest.

Among the new arrivals in November appeared another Englishman, Captain John Starr, who was placed in a hut with the Frenchmen he had accompanied by cattletruck from Saarbrucken shortly before the American Army's arrival there. Starr was a mystery man from SOE, a fluent French linguist with a good knowledge of German who had been caught behind the German lines and was vague about his subsequent interrogation and treatment. Naturally he kept his secrets to himself, and for the same reason Godwin was careful when they were introduced to give only the barest outline of his background for fear Starr was an SS plant. With wry humour, however, Godwin could safely describe their march which was close to a year in length of time and over the 10,000-mile mark. 'The distance from Berlin to New York, from New York back to Berlin and halfway across the Atlantic again', he remarked with pride. Starr would not be put in the SK compound, yet at once was made to march in the SK which came as a frightful shock since, for nearly a year, he had been locked in a cell and had hardly walked at all—or so he claimed.

Christmas came and went, the illuminated tree standing once more on Tyburn, the Norwegians as determined as ever to celebrate as lavishly as possible (and managing to defy a total ban imposed by the SS), slightly under a cloud, since the final German offensive in the West had recently made a big dent in the Allied lines in the Ardennes and nobody was yet sure how much longer this would prolong the war and reduce their own chances of early release. But Sachsenhausen, of course, was ever a place of paradoxes. Just a fortnight before Christmas Eve, Nansen had been regretting the manner in which his own countrymen, who were in possession of considerable stocks of food parcels, were 'bargaining and scrounging', but not *giving*.

> 'Thus it is only the fittest and the smart who get anything. . . . It's the Ukrainian, the Russian, the Pole who takes the whole risk, and who is hanged or punished if its found out. . . . The Norwegian owner of sardines, ham, cheese, butter, sausage, tobacco and all the good things that makes life here liveable and bearable goes scot-free.'

It was this food, thought Nansen, which really placed the Norwegians on a special footing in the camp, which now transcended the ruling qualities of German, racial superiority, and which, incidentally, now absolved Norwegians from beatings.

When it had become a common chore to cart away frozen bodies after each cold January night, and as news of the collapse of the Ardennes offensive circulated, horrors multiplied incredibly. While the brothel alongside the hospital did a roaring trade (with even the emaciated queuing eagerly for a 20 minute session), so-called 'death gangs' of saboteurs and looters from Berlin were formed and billeted alongside the SK. Thus the CHECKMATE party, trudging their routine in bitter weather, were compelled to look upon all manner of men, and even young lads, significant black crosses painted upon their faces waiting their end. Among the 'death gangs' suffered Jewish boys who, by some miracle, had survived the holocaust visited upon the majority of their race who had fallen into German hands. Savagely violated by the several homosexual guards among the camp staff, they would soon be driven with shouts of '*Raus! Raus!*' to the *Sonderwagen*—the latest, most sinister, arrival from the East—from Chelmno, where it had played a relatively small part in gassing Jews by carbon monoxide pumped into its lorries' sealed containers. Yet the toll exacted by this inefficient process was as nothing compared with the deaths from cold, pneumonia and starvation among tens of thousands now on the road, flooding in ahead of the Russians as they drove towards the Oder and Berlin. By the score the dead were pulled from the railway trucks, collapsed by the wayside and died unattended.

It is a tribute to Godwin's extraordinary feat in keeping them going and to the Norwegian's steadfastness that the CHECKMATE party had remained in fairly good trim, with its morale intact, and that only now did the first crack appear. It was also a tribute to Alfred Roe that, as the least dedicated and easily the oldest among them, he stayed the course as long as he did. Even at this stage, when he began to fail, very few knew of his distress. His comrades became worried because he was beginning to curry favour with the guards, thus posing a security risk to British and Norwegians alike. There is a report on file saying that serious consideration was given about the middle of January to eliminating the danger by having Roe killed. Obviously this suggestion received scant examination. For one thing, it would have been a betrayal of a member of the *prominenten* by the *prominenten* itself. For another, a relapse into the abysmal standards of their captors. Anyway, there was a better way out, by transferring him to the hospital, even though he was in outstandingly good health compared with the majority crowding that dreadful camp as it approached the awful climax of its existence, and Musselmen died on its steps without the remotest chance of receiving attention.

20

The Panic

The hospital (*Revier*) did duty as a haven of order on the threshold of sanity within the mad complex of Sachsenhausen. Since the day when it was part of a showplace among concentration camps, it had been well equipped with X-ray machines, two operating theatres and a laboratory and now it reflected Norwegian authoritativeness under the direction of their doctors and male nurses—to the exclusion of SS staff who ran their own establishment which occasionally carried out bizarre experiments on prisoners, including those of German nationality. Admission to the *Revier* was open to all nationalities, including the senior SS member of the camp staff whom a few gloating Norwegians were invited to observe as he lay in the last agonies of cancer. Like nearly everything else, however, a bed in the *Revier* had to be 'organised'. Indeed, Kunke's fall had been brought about through his involvement in 'organising' the admission of a friend. Medical supplies, including even penicillin, were obtained from Red Cross sources and from the Germans. Once a month Alf Aadnoy would visit the Head of Medical Supplies in Berlin to place a requisition. There, amid the ruins, he could see the extreme effect of people's apathy and benefit from their bureaucrats' version of 'rowing' in a city persistently under air raid alert. For Aadnoy discovered that it was only necessary to mention to obstructive officials the retribution impending when the war was over to have them approve the most extortionate requisition for drugs. Food remained the staple of exchange throughout the camp system, but the threat of a return to natural justice was beginning to work wonders.

Alfred Roe—called Walter by Rolf Skauger, one of the nurses—found shelter in a crowded ward of the *Revier*. In mid-January he had reported sick with a high temperature and lung trouble which, as Skauger says, was a trivial complaint in the circumstances. Like most of the *prominenten*, Roe was fairly well fed and, in the CHECKMATE tradition, fit, cheerful and joking all the time. It was his morale which had collapsed. When they found the opportunity to converse, Roe unburdened himself to Skauger of what must have been a long-pent-up discontent. He expressed his dissatisfaction with the planning and execution of the raid on Kopervik, regretting, with a laugh, that he had volunteered—as volunteers whose folly has caught up with them ironically

138

tend to do. No doubt a short breather in the *Revier* with time to recover his composure would have seen Roe through to the end. But the Russians put an end to that when they arrived at the River Oder and the news broke in camp that they had crossed near Kustrin, only 40 kilometres distant, and were heading for Berlin, Oranienburg and Sachsenhausen.

On 31 January, the 12th anniversary of his coming to power, Hitler broadcast to his people for the last time, prophesying the Russians would be stopped. Only fanatics and madmen believed him, as a fiery rumour swept through the camp that evacuation was imminent and that next day its 40,000 or more inhabitants would be joining the migration from the East, piling chaos upon chaos in a disaster out of control. In a state of considerable euphoria, the Norwegians, the British and all non-Musselmen, whose better health and spirits harboured a belief in rescue, prepared to depart, selecting what they must carry, putting aside the few things that would be useless.

Many people have covered more than 30 miles in a single day carrying 40 lb, and not a few have kept it up for a week or so at a stretch without collapsing from exhaustion. But it is doubtful if anybody has marched anything like 12,500 miles in just short of 420 days consecutively when frequently deprived of a good night's sleep, living in squalor and with a food intake close to the threshold of sufficiency. But, with the exception of Alfred Roe, whose performance had fallen only just short, that is what the CHECKMATE party had achieved when they were dismissed from the trackway on the evening of 2 February. That night the party began their customary round of friends, wondering if this might be the last occasion it would be necessary to do so, thrilled with the prospect of a change if not yet rescue.

Shortly before midnight the first signs of unusual activity by the SS gave credence to the rumours as a bevy of officers, most of them drunk, entered the SK compound and began to shout the names of selected prisoners, prefaced by the placatory yet ominous instructions: 'Do not bother to bring anything with you. Everything necessary will be taken care of where you are going.'

The Panic, as it came to be known, had started, triggered by instructions from Oranienburg to destroy key witnesses and evidence of the kind most likely to incriminate the SS in the postwar world of Allied retribution.

It was an event everybody, and most of all people of special category such as Godwin and his crew, had foreseen as a likely climax amid the closing days of the Third Reich. Only recently, John Godwin had discussed the prospects with a Norwegian friend, Martin Holmens, and had said that he and his men would, if possible, put up resistance if sent to 'stand by the gate' on their way to the 'Transports', the place of execution in the *Industriehof* near the crematorium.

'Our Prime Minister, Winston Churchill, had a catch phrase in 1940 when the Germans were expected to invade us, you know. It was "Take one with you". Well, so far, I can tell you, none of us have "taken a single one". We sank a trawler, yes, but that's all. Maybe I managed to shoot down an aeroplane, though I rather doubt it. So I'm damned if after all this I don't make at least one of these monsters suffer.'

Godwin did not specify how it would be done, but by the quiet, assured tone Holmens was left in no doubt that a determined operation had been planned and discussed by the entire British party.

Only Roe, in the *Revier*, and Mayor did not answer when the SS began calling out the names not only of the CHECKMATE party but also those of many more. Elsewhere the same procedure was being followed with inordinate haste, those selected and told to 'report to the gate' drawn from several nationalities and including, to everyone's surprise, some hated creatures of the Gestapo, the sycophantic prisoners who had helped keep order by spying upon their fellows. Not until a little before midnight had the entire group—some put it at four to five hundred—assembled under the arclights at the gate, each by now consumed by dread. Yet only a handful, as was almost invariably the case among a concentration camp's doomed, were steeled to put up a fight. Apathy, absence of a coordinating determined leadership, as well as lack of opportunity or weapons, usually militated against resistance. So the SS tended to grow careless and only rarely, if that carelessness overlooked a bunch of desperate victims who were trained fighting men under firm leadership, did the long compressed powder keg of hatred explode.

Time to insert the fuse was provided by the Royal Air Force. Before the assembly was complete, the air raid sirens blew and the lights, as usual, were switched off, thus preventing the march to the *Industriehof*. For nearly four hours they waited in the dark and in that time Godwin was able to organise his men thoroughly and allocate them key positions and tasks, poised to take advantage of the slightest lapse by the guards when the lights came on, the gates were opened and they started marching, right handed, towards the factory buildings. During that respite, when their stomachs churned from an excitement rivalling the fear clutching at their hearts, they must have been delighted to find among their companions, the vast majority of whom were stunned by the close proximity of oblivion, an élite like themselves for whom the drama of the moment was a challenge to action. Of these, the Poles were outstanding, one of whom, it is believed, was armed with a knife. Optimism no doubt had its final fling. Maybe there were those who even imagined a miraculous deliverance. But as they were led away, Godwin was heard to shout: 'They have taken everything from us but not our spirit. God save the King!'

Meanwhile Keith Mayor, whose name had apparently been left off the list and who had gone to bed, awoke amid the turmoil and learnt what was happening. His first act was to dress and his next to write a short note to his family which he handed to a Norwegian friend, Leif Jensen. Scrawled in pencil and bearing the appalling strain of the moment it read:

'Dearest Mother and Father and all, all my love and hoping you will not forget your only son.

God bless you all and God Save the King.

Yours ever,

Keith   XXX

Then he made a determined move to join his comrades at the gate to share their fate in the way they had shared everything the past two years. Several people expostulated, saying the sacrifice was unnecessary. Joining with them was *Blockälteste* Jakob whose conscience cracked this night. He insisted that Mayor must hide with some others, including a few Dutchmen, in hut 58.

What happened after the lights came on is confused by the many fragmentary accounts. It could hardly have been otherwise in such a moment of terror. There is evidence that the SS discovered Mayor was missing and made an unavailing search for him. It is clear, too, that as the condemned moved through the gate, their shouting, singing and jostling created the distraction required by Godwin and permitted him to close with one of the drunken, unwary guards to snatch the man's weapon and shoot him. Immediately the armed Pole stabbed another guard and this was the signal for a small dedicated group of British and Poles, perhaps with a few Russians, to band together in a spontaneous uprising of the greatest rarity in the circumstances; to seize two or three more guards, along with their weapons, and bundle them into a nearby factory building.

The astonishment of the befuddled SS can easily be imagined. They were not accustomed to resistance. Those who kept their heads seem to have managed to keep the majority of the crowd prisoners moving towards their final destination. One or two opened fire indiscriminately, listeners inside the camp noticing how the uproar outside contained an irregularity of firing compared to previous 'orderly' executions. Not all of it came at once from the usual place near the crematorium. The evidence, sketchily composed over the ensuing days from badly shaken guards and from the observations of Norwegians, points to a few determined souls managing to break into one of the factory buildings. There, presumably to conserve ammunition, and as the by-product of two years' pent-up savagery, they took revenge by kicking into unconsciousness (some say to death) two or three guards. Armed with but a few captured firearms, it was possible only to put the building into a token state of defence, never with a real hope of escape. It is possible to conjure up a vision of John Godwin, face lit up by a transient victory, with controlled ferocity and staunchly backed up by his followers, hunting for more victims in dark places until the arrival of SS reinforcements turned him into the hunted, and as they were one by one cornered and shot down. There would have been no mercy from either side. In this, the first and last battle of the CHECKMATE party's existence, quarter, like its good fortune, would have been at a premium.

Rolf Skauger says that shooting went on in a sporadic manner for about $1\frac{1}{2}$ hours. Some of that firing would have come from the execution of the more passive prisoners. But clearly the rest came from the assault on Godwin's party and their last stand.

Before daylight the racket had subsided, although, quite obviously, the normal state of affairs was gone forever. Turmoil would flourish. It was mid-day before the Germans finished clearing up the mess and permitted routine activity in the *Industriehof*. By then it was generally known that the British were dead. Some people had seen their bloodstained and torn clothing laid out. There was a great sense of shock and loss and, as Nansen wrote 'the atmosphere filled with gloom'. When Skauger told Roe in the *Revier*, the Petty Officer wept. But at the same time Skauger insisted that Roe must be smuggled out of Sachsenhausen at once to escape the same fate when the SS realised they had missed one of the men who 'had to be killed because they knew too much about the illegal maltreatment of prisoners'.

> 'We will register you as a Norwegian' [Skauger said] 'and arrange for you to join a party who are due to go tomorrow to a rest camp. It's some distance to the West, but closer to your own countrymen—which may be an advantage in due course. It's a place called Belsen.'

It was done. Two days later Roe was crammed into a railway truck, lonely and shaken, yet happy to have escaped to a place which could not, by any stretch of imagination, be worse than Sachsenhausen.

John Starr was also lucky. Jean Overton Fuller, in her apologia for Starr, *The Starr Affair*, in which she attempts to defend him against charges of having betrayed his contacts in the SOE in France to the Germans, explains how he met Jakob, who talked with shame of what had happened the previous night. He said the British had been hanged from hooks, that it was murder and a disgrace to Germany. There is no authentication of this that I can find, and I doubt its veracity, although in the stress and fury of the moment, brought about by the slaying of their comrades, the SS were capable of anything. Beyond much doubt, however, Jakob was severely shocked, the account of his cursing and tears of remorse ringing true of a man trapped by his own sins. For Jakob, the Army deserter now copied Skauger by insisting to Starr that the SS 'will come again for you'. And the Norwegians, who agreed, also took Starr in hand, fitting him into a party consigned to Multhausen, a camp with a reputation, had they but known it, as bad as, if not worse than, that of Sachsenhausen.

Starr would survive Multhausen and return to England and France to face protracted investigation and to tell his tale. Roe and Mayor also escaped, the former getting away on the 4th, the latter on the 8th to wend their way by cattle truck in the company, respectively, of Norwegians and Dutchmen, to be thrust out upon the long platform at Bergen Belsen railway yard. Here they were reintroduced to a scene which was familiar, although already catastrophically far worse even than Sachsenhausen. Marched among hundreds to a wired-in hutted camp set among pine trees, they found themselves amid overcrowding of tens of thousands afflicted by unprecedented conditions of malnutrition and disease.

Here but few Red Cross parcels were available, and nearly everybody suffered from the decline in 'resting metabolic rate', reducing them to skeletal Musselmen as their bodies fed upon their own tissues. Here the death role soared to 300 per day, from the commonly associated pulmonary troubles and from typhus whose outbreak practically coincided with the arrival of the CHECKMATE survivors. From that moment onward the inflow of refugees from all over the shrinking Third Reich completely overwhelmed the camp's administration, a state of chaos and deprivation compounded by the incompetence and indifference of its commandant, Josef Kramer, who had previously worked at Auschwitz under Rudolf Hoess, the man who, it will be recalled, was the instigator of the rotten, criminal system at Sachsenhausen in 1939.

Everything possible was done by Mayor's and Roe's friends to conceal their identity. At the suggestion of an Austrian prisoner, Rolf Klink, Mayor was registered as Dutch and in this guise he survived amid the death from disease until mid-March; seeing the bodies pile up, hearing the rattle of shots when the guards riddled would-be escapers with bullets; sharing what little food he had with friends—like them all, progressively becoming weaker than at any time since entering captivity. It was much the same for Roe, but it was Mayor who first began to suffer from stomach troubles and a high temperature, and soon to admit to Klink, 'I feel I have got typhus.' Next morning he was sent to hospital block 17 where the disease engulfed him and he was fed and nursed by Dr Leo and several other Sachsenhausen friends amidst the foul squalor of the over-crowded building. The crisis broke on 25 March, with a temperature of 40°C and he held on to life.

Towards the end of the month, however, Klink was ordered to find two 'numbers', meaning prisoners,

'saying that they had forgotten to send these two for a transport. I called the chiefs of the blocks, asking them if they had people of this number. The chief of Block 17 said "He is here, but he has got typhus." It was then that I remembered that this number was Keith's number. I went back to Emmerich and told him "One number we have. The man is in hospital with typhus and cannot go." He said, "Is he very ill?" I said, Yes".'

Later that day, according to Dr Leo (who as a fellow prisoner had known Mayor in Sachsenhausen), the SS Dr Horstmann 'came into our hospital and asked where the bed of Keith Mayor was. He was shown and went and examined the patient superficially, something which he had never done before.'

That evening, 11 April, Klink was told to fetch Mayor. A new *Unterscharfuhrer* called Wolf, dressed in a black rubber coat, was in attendance and it was he who now told Klink to write down Mayor's name and date of birth. 'Mayor held my hand to support himself and whispered his name, date and month and year. . . . Keith said, "I know you love England. When you get there tell them the truth".' Under oath, Klink would be better than his word, as would a Frenchman called Max Markowicz, who, in his deposition, confirmed Wolf's name and recorded seeing Mayor's body lying on a heap of straw near the kitchen with his arms outstretched and a small pistol bullet hole in the centre of his forehead. Dr Leo, in evidence at the trial of Kramer and 44 others, would attest that the execution took place in the room of *Blockführer* Stuber.

Alfred Roe was spared Mayor's treatment. He simply died along with many others from typhus, intercepted from survival in the perverse style of the entire CHECKMATE party, within either an ace of real success or a few hours of rescue. Less than 4 days after Mayor was killed, the advance guard of the British Army reached Belsen.

It was not known how it came about that the SS came to learn of the presence of Roe and Mayor at Belsen, but it is not beyond much doubt that orders did come from the political department at Oranienburg to the political department at Belsen under *Obersturmführer* Friedrich, to eliminate the last of the CHECKMATE party whose evidence after the war would have led to many convictions for breach of the Geneva Convention.

21

The Telling of the Saga

It was rather typical of the ironies accumulating round the CHECKMATE party that six weeks after they had been killed their families received news through the Red Cross that they were alive but in considerable danger. It was the first official notification in 21 months. Several close relatives, including Godwin's father and twin brother and Cox's mother, had come to believe their men were dead. Mrs Cox had been convinced by a nightmare on or about the night that he was killed fighting in the *Industriehof*. She had described it at once to her daughter, who was sharing her bed that night. She had seen Jack crouched in the corner of a cage. He had said 'Oh, Mum. I'm cold', and she had covered him with her coat and then woken up. At that moment she gave up hope. Yet it was the women, above all the mothers, who mostly clung to hope, although it was mightily disconcerting to learn that their men were in danger and no attempt made to contact them. By mid-March the war in Europe was very clearly on its last legs as the Allied armies converged from all points of the compass. So there was some consolation that it was only a question of waiting before a telegram of good cheer, a voice on the telephone, best of all a knock on the door, made everything come right. So confident was Neville Burgess's mother that each night she left the door unlatched so that he could walk in without knocking. Moreover, she continued to leave it open as May gave way to June, and even after the letters announcing that each man must be presumed lost began to arrive.

From the Norwegians came the sorry tale of what had taken place in Sachsenhausen, with an outline of what had happened between May 1943 and that final confrontation on the night of 2 February 1945. Between the night of the shooting and the end of the war, the Norwegians had undergone traumas of their own, shunted westward on foot or in cattle wagons to camps as horrifying as they had experienced previously, losing some of their number until eventually those with enough strength and fortitude were saved by the Swedes who were permitted to send in missions to evacuate their fellow Scandinavians as the Third Reich fell in chaos to its long awaited conquerers.

In Sachsenhausen, where a limited amount of time could be spared by the living for the dead, much effort had to be spent on survival. With hundreds dying it was scarcely possible to mourn the passing of one person before another took his place. As a sickening result, it was only close friends who could be given more than passing sympathy and who would be remembered by name. Therefore, it is remarkable the manner in which the CHECKMATE party were mourned, the way nearly all surviving Norwegians remembered them as if they were personal friends, and the consistency with which the Britons' closest of comrades kept faith by taking immense trouble to inform the authorities and carry messages, even across the world, to Argentina and Newfoundland.

Within a week of the war's end, detailed reports via the Military Attaché, Stockholm, had been received from Fenrik Rosenquist and from Leif Jensen, the latter enclosing Keith Mayor's last letter. Jensen's letter was, indeed, impressive, yet it contained several inaccuracies based upon unfounded hearsay, including the totally false suggestion that there was reason to believe Captain Starr had been shot at Multhausen. In the months to come most, if not all, of the families received one or more visits or letters from Norwegian or Dutch friends pledged to a proud duty.

The first letters to arrive, however, were the official ones from Admiralty and War Office. They gave the confirmation that the men concerned had been killed, expressing deep regret and condolences and completing the legal formalities demanded of the occasion. In the circumstances it is difficult to see what else the bureaucracy could do, since the CHECKMATE party were but a few among thousands of the missing who had now to be presumed dead or unaccounted for. Not all the next of kin were content to leave it at that, however. As a result of the trial in 1945 of Kramer, the story that Keith Mayor had been killed in Sachsensenhausen (as one paper said) or Belsen (in the correct words of another) received publicity. His mother therefore wrote in September to the Admiralty requesting details, and a month later received a reply saying he had been captured on a secret operation in Norway; that he was not a paratrooper; that nothing had been heard of him until March 1945, when he was reported in German hands; that initially two reports had said he was shot at Sachsenhausen on 2 February, but subsequently it appeared he had been shot at Belsen. Apparently the officer who signed the letter was unaware of the 1943 and 1944 reports indicating Mayor was alive then. Or was it a cover-up demanded by regulations which, arguably for security reasons, could not disclose information obtained from secret sources in time of war? But the war was now over.

The rules of secrecy also plagued Mrs Burgess when she asked a local solicitor at Beverley, who was engaged in the prosecution of Nazi War Criminals, if he could discover anything. He did manage to obtain the gist of the story for her, but stipulated that she must keep it to herself. So persuasive was her respect for regulations, she decided not even to tell her husband for fear he let it slip in the pub, nor did she tell all the rest of the family for many years later, with the result that it was not until I was researching this book that Neville Burgess's brothers and sisters heard of his gallantry.

Gallantry was officially mentioned in the case of two of them. In October 1945 John Godwin posthumously was awarded a Mention in Despatches 'for great gallantry at Sachsenhausen'; and two years later Keith Mayor received a similar posthumous award for 'endurance and great fortitude'. Somebody had remembered. And, in due course, in two instalments paid for as reparations by the German government to UK victims of Nazi persecution, the families received fairly substantial sums of money.

Efforts were made to bring those responsible for the treatment of the CHECKMATE party to justice, but in the circumstances it proved impossible to deal with them all. Hitler, Himmler and many of those reponsible for SS policy were either dead, missing or arraigned on appropriate charges. Kramer and his underlings were tried, executed or imprisoned. The same applied to a few of the lower orders belonging to camp staffs, although those responsible at Sachsenhausen were either dead or untraceable. The Norwegians did get their hands on the drunken Seidler and gave him a long sentence in gaol. In this context it is ironic that almost the first non-official letter received by the Godwin family in Argentina came from a man claiming to be the German officer who had captured Godwin and the rest. He said his orders had been to shoot them, but this he could not do. Therefore he circumvented this order by issuing them with Norwegian documents and packing them off to a civilian concentration camp instead of a prisoner-of-war camp. This, of course, was a gross oversimplification and a fabrication explainable by reason of the German's personal difficulties. He wrote that he had been a schoolmaster before the war and he was now anxious to return to work, but first had to be cleared by a de-Nazification court. So would the Godwins please supply a testimony that he had treated him and his men properly? Clearly that was impossible and it was not done. He sent to the Godwins the two photographs reproduced between pages 96 and 97 showing himself with the party just after their capture, one shot quite clearly showing that they were properly dressed with Royal Navy shoulder flashes.

After the publicity about Keith Mayor in 1945 and until the rules governing relaxation of access to official documents in the Public Record Office, London, in the early 1970s, the CHECKMATE story was virtually forgotten. It was excluded from the official histories and what few mentions it received in books about commandos tended to express ignorance of what had occurred. That is, until a book called *Undercover Sailors* by A. Cecil Hampshire was published in 1981, in which a complete chapter was devoted to 'The Tragedy of Operation "Checkmate"'. Mr Hampshire, late of the Royal Navy and a journalist, carried out exhaustive research into the official records. Unfortunately, when it came to its application he failed to relate the information accurately to the maps and charts and made virtually no effort to follow up his research, to fill gaps in the official documents or to resolve the problems raised, several of which were of his own making.

Despite the provision of coordinates of latitude and longitude in the orders and reports acquired by Mr Hampshire, the map in his book contains such glaring errors as the omission of the Urter island from off the north-west coast of Karmoy. In the text, he stated that Sussart (*sic*) is 'at the southern end of Karmoy' (instead of where it actually is on the mainland) and proved it to his own satisfaction (presumably) by inserting that phrase in the translation of the German documents. As a result of these misconceptions, among others, and because he apparently made no effort to trace the sequence of action or visit its scene, he compiled a faulty account and drew conclusions which, by implication, are damaging to Godwin's reputation. But since the entire chapter devoted to CHECKMATE is a hotchpotch of unrelated chunks from the official documents, it is preferable to leave it at that — except perhaps to suggest that, in all probability, the sagas of old include similar distortions.

Towards the end of 1982 there was further journalistic coverage in a three-part serial by a Lancashire evening paper concentrating upon Keith Mayor's side of the story. As with the Hampshire chapter, useful research had been done, but without any constructive attempt to piece together the whole tale or get to the root of the matter.

My interest in CHECKMATE was stimulated while carrying out research in the Public Record Office, Kew, into the wider field of amphibious hit-and-run raiding. Thereafter, by a combination of curiosity and coincidence after I made initial, tentative inquiries in Norway, I was simply overwhelmed by help and kindness from numerous Norwegians who, in one place or another, had met with and shared the perils of the British commandos. In addition, I sought and received considerable assistance from individuals and organisations in Britain. The names of most of them will be familiar to readers of this book. To all the participants I extend my heartfelt thanks for their immense generosity in all manner of ways and the wonderfully moving effusions of gratitude in helping me compose the story of the CHECKMATE party of whom they have such indelible memories and admiration. To some extent they have also contributed to a record of their own achievements in terrible circumstances. In listing below all those who contributed, I do so in the realisation that I may have accidentally omitted one or two helpers (and of them I crave forgiveness) and that many now deceased would have liked to have said their piece.

In the region of the Sognefjord and the Shetland Isles
  Rear Admiral Charles Herlofson, DSC
  Leif Utne
  Kenyon Waggett

In the region of Karmoy and Stavanger
  Jacob Børresen
  Alf Aadnoy, who was also in Grini and Sachsenhausen, and who, through
    Stavanger Aftenblad, put me in touch with:
  The Pederson brothers
  Erling Jøssang
  Kjell Øverland

At Grini and Sachsenhausen
  Arne Herwander
  Martin Holmens
  Rolf Skauger

Members of the families involved
  The Godwin family
  The Cox family
  The Burgess family
  The Mayor family
  Tim Greve, on behalf of the Nansen family, who through his newspaper put
    me in contact with Sachsenhausen survivors, granted me permission to
    reproduce copies of his father-in-law's pictures and advised me on certain
    aspects of that invaluable diary of Odd Nansen, *Day after Day*.

Individuals providing source material or expert advice
  The Naval Historical Branch, Ministry of Defence, London
  The Public Record Office
  The Imperial War Museum
  Knut Haukelid, formerly of the Resistance Museum, Oslo

With the information received from these sources, it has been possible, I
estimate, to reduce the amount of conjectural material to about 5 per cent of the
whole text. And wherever I felt compelled to resort to conjecture, I was
governed by what that admirable historian, Alfred Burn, called IMP—Inherent Military Probability—by relating the imagined behaviour and remarks by
some of the people in certain situations to their authenticated characteristics in
similar circumstances. This I have done purely in the interests of storytelling
without the slightest intention of warping the account by overdramatisation.